The Emerging Self

by

Ernest C. Wilson

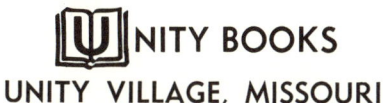

UNITY BOOKS
UNITY VILLAGE, MISSOURI

Standard Book Number 87159-137-5

Library of Congress Card Number 75-120119

Dedicated to
The Emerging Man

Of his own will he brought us forth by the word of truth that we should be a kind of first fruits of his creatures.

—James 1:18.

Contents

Author's Note

Something that I would be tempted to call "one of life's little miracles" happened while I was writing this book. It has to do with the portrait that appears on the cover.

About a year ago, a California friend, who was a member of a teen-agers' Sunday-school class that I taught in Kansas City years ago, wrote and told me she was painting a portrait of me, and that she hoped to send it to me before Christmas.

I was working to complete the manuscript on this book, and had set myself a January deadline. As the manuscript approached completion and the publishers wanted a title, I settled on *The Emerging Self* as my choice.

A few days before Christmas, the painting arrived. I opened the crate in which it was carefully packed with some trepidation, as a really fine portrait is a rare thing. I was delighted to see what an excellent painting the artist had achieved. Others who saw it were equally impressed. One of them said, "Why, it's a portrayal of your book title, *The Emerging Self!*" Surely it seemed so.

The artist did not know what I was writing, and no title had been determined. It was one of life's little miracles that we cannot explain otherwise than as coincidence or inspiration.

The artist, known to her friends as Geneva Hall Daniel, signs her work "Leonarda." The painting now hangs in the narthex of Unity Temple on the Country Club Plaza in Kansas City, Missouri, where once again I serve as minister after an interval of nearly thirty years.

Ernest C. Wilson

Acknowledgments

Unless otherwise stated, Scriptural passages are from the Revised Standard Version of the Bible, published by Thomas Nelson and Sons, New York.

Masaharu Taniguchi, *You Can Heal Yourself* and *Recovery from All Diseases,* Seicho-No-Ie Foundation, Tokyo, Japan.

Sir Edwin Arnold, *The Light of Asia,* Robert Bros., Boston.

T. R. Glover, *The Jesus of History,* Association Press, New York.

Curtis Vaughan, *The New Testament from 26 Translations,* Zondervan Publishing House, Grand Rapids, Mich.

J. R. Dummelow, *One Volume Bible Commentary,* Macmillan, New York.

James Morgan Pryse, *The Restored New Testament,* John M. Watkins, London.

A. Milton Smith, *The Twelve Apostles,* Fleming H. Revell, New York.

J. W. Dunne, *An Experiment with Time,* Macmillan, New York.

Arthur Christopher Benson, *Child of the Dawn,* Falcon's Wing Press, Indian Hills, Colo.

P. D. Ouspensky, *Tertium Organum,* Alfred A. Knopf, New York.

Pierre Teilhard de Chardin, *The Phenomenon of Man,* Harper and Brothers, New York.

Frederick D. Leete, *Christianity in Science,* Abingdon Press, New York.

Edwin E. Slosson, *Sermons of a Chemist,* Harcourt, Brace and Co., New York.

Catherine Ponder, *Healing Secrets of the Ages,* Parker Publishing Co., New York.

Alexis Carrel, *Prayer,* Hodder and Stoughton, London.

Edward Carpenter, *Towards Democracy,* George Allen and Unwin, London.

Charles Fillmore, Unity Books, Unity Village, Mo.
Atom-Smashing Power of Mind
Talks on Truth
Prosperity
Keep a True Lent
Twelve Powers of Man

H. Emilie Cady, *Lessons in Truth,* Unity Books, Unity Village, Mo.

Imelda Octavia Shanklin, *What Are You?* Unity Books, Unity Village, Mo.

Introduction

The Human Predicament

Why are we here? What is the purpose of life? Why is there so much evil in the world? Why do the wicked prosper, the righteous suffer? Why, as the poet put it, is "Right forever on the scaffold, Wrong forever on the throne"?

Is man the helpless victim of fate or chance? Has he been thrust helpless into an alien world where the forces of life are pitted against him, doomed to a few short years of youth and growth, followed by a decline of his physical and mental forces, often accompanied by illness, suffering, perhaps privation, culminating in death and extinction?

Is this the best we can hope for? Our despair asserts it. Our hope denies it. What can a man believe? Where can he place his trust?

Somewhere in the remote past, apparently mankind demanded to learn by experience rather than by precept. He left the security of a guided life and set out to have his own way.

The story is an old one.

Plato depicts a man chained in an underground cavern, whose only light is from an open fire. He is chained so that he cannot see the fire or the other occupants of the cave. He sees men as shadows reflected on the wall he faces. Finally he rebels. He breaks his chains and gropes his way by a winding stair to the light of the upper world. He staggers and stumbles like one suddenly become blind. But his blindness is not the blindness of light that is lost, but light that is found.

The Tree of Desire

Moses tells about a couple who lived in a lovely garden where everything was done for them. They were "naked, and were not ashamed." That is, they had no thoughts apart from their Maker. Then they "ate of the fruit" of the tree of desire, and wanted to hide their thoughts and keep them to themselves. So they made themselves aprons because "they knew that they were naked."

They intended to dress the garden and keep it. Instead they dressed themselves and lost the garden, or were thereby evicted from it! From then on they had to work and earn their keep by the sweat of their brows.

There was both a gain and a loss involved. Ever since, mankind has tried to find or create such a garden and return to it, but has not succeeded.

Jesus tells much the same story but with a happier ending. You know the story, if not from the Bible then from one of the scores of novels and plays that have been derived from it—such a play as "The Wanderer" in which William Collier and Nance O'Neill were featured.

As Jesus tells the story, a youth grew restless in his father's house, demanded his inheritance. He took it, and went into a far country where he spent his substance in "loose living." His fair-weather friends deserted him one by one as his fortune diminished. Finally he was reduced to about as low a state as Jesus could picture to the Jewish people to whom He told the story. The impetuous youth was reduced to feeding swine—swine that were anathema to the Jews. And "he would gladly have fed on the pods that the swine ate."

Finally "he came to himself," and a bright though not too welcome thought came to him. "I will arise and go to my father," he said to himself–not too welcome an impulse because of his feeling of guilt. He had asked a lot of his father, had been given a lot, and then had frittered it away foolishly. He had gained experience, but he had lost a lot too; his home, his security, his father's love perhaps. He felt guilty, and if a man has a sense of guilt, somehow he always seems to feel that he must be punished. He attributes expected punishment to God, but he decrees it to himself.

A Sense of Guilt

From the first dawning of human consciousness that seems to have been the case. If man did not feel guilty there always seemed to be something to *make* him feel so. When the thunder roared and the lightning flashed, he took these to be signs of the displeasure of some unseen higher power which must be propitiated. A volcanic eruption was serious not only because it destroyed people, their meager possessions, and the products of the earth, but as an indication of the extremity of a god's displeasure. That power must be appeased. Man must make some sacrifice. What did he value most? A human life? That of a child, or a young woman?

Somehow such ideas have persisted down to the present era. No earlier than the turn of the century when the San Francisco earthquake and resultant fire destroyed so much of the great city, many devout people attributed the disaster to God's displeasure with the immorality and vice of the district known as the Barbary Coast.

Our prodigal son suffered from this sense of guilt more than from his deprivations. Now he thought (with dread we may be sure) of the recrimination and punishments he must endure, the utter humiliation of facing his family, the good brother who had stayed home, and his father whose love he had betrayed. Fearfully he started on the way back to his father's house. But as Jesus tells us, while the youth was still a long way off, his father saw him coming and rejoiced at his return. No element of punishment or reproach! Prepare a feast, get a fine robe for his body, a ring for his finger! Welcome, welcome! "For this my son was dead, and is alive again; he was lost, and is found."

If you feel close to Jesus, you might have expected that His story would be the best of all, the most explicit, the most significant and revealing. And it is.

He points the way out of the human predicament.

Defiance or a Plea

When in their anguish, which often wears the mask of defiance, men cry out "There is no God!" one may get the intimation of a plea. As when someone tells you he is an agnostic, or even an atheist, you may feel that without consciously realizing the fact, he is actually longing to be convinced that there is indeed a God and hopes that you can help to convince him.

This is the great need of all time, and especially of this time.

We can no longer accept many of the old concepts of God: the stern father, the great king on a throne—surrounded, unhappily, by twenty-four beasts and elders—or a judge passing sentence upon timorous souls, guilt-laden, who appear before Him.

The real intent of Jesus' story of the prodigal son is pretty much obscured by the figure He employed. Comparing God to a father is a great tribute to Joseph, the forgotten man of the New Testament, but it is not always a happy comparison for modern man. Today man has become wary of the father-figure—well-meaning, no doubt, but often as insecure, as filled with doubts, as are his children; no safe guide in a world of splitting atoms, splitting factions among people who we feel should get along together because there are enough disturbances in the world already, without that!

Yes, somewhere in the remote past man chose the way of experience rather than guidance. He is convinced—too well—that he is a son of earth, aware of his kinship to what it pleases him to call the lower creation. Is the evidence not all too plain that the human fetus repeats in fine the story of evolution, from single cell to fish to monkey to man? Does he not even bear in the structure of his adult body the remnants of the simian tail?

All this is almost painfully evident to man, so much so that it may be a long while before he finds the grace (if he ever does) to acknowledge how much he owes to that lower creation for its contributions to the body that man inhabits. Not, perhaps, until the awareness, or the longing, comes upon him that he is more than flesh, and that earth is not his home; that he is indeed the prodigal of whom Jesus told us, who has wandered off into a far country, and has become so mesmerized by it and its demands and allurements and problems and responsibilities that the remembrance of who and what he truly is is all but submerged and lost.

When he begins to be aware of the limitations of the physical world and of his physical nature—wonderful though they are—and starts searching for something that will give him a needed sense of purpose and fulfillment, then he may think of trying to find a power higher than the self he knows. He begins a quest for truth, he wants to "find God." But one seeks to find only what is lost, and God is not lost. We are. Or rather our awareness of our oneness with Him is lost. We "come to ourself," to use Jesus' term, and try to find our way back "home." Often the poets are wayfinders and wayshowers. It was one of them who cried, "I'm homesick for a land I have not seen!"

To our human sense the way back is a long, long way. To tell a person who is just awakening to the sense of the Self beyond self (the World beyond worlds) that it is "nearer than breathing, closer than hands and feet," seems an empty assurance. And though "the far is near, and the future is near," it does not *seem* so. Between what man sees himself to be, and what he aspires to be, there is "a great chasm." "The gate is narrow and the way is hard . . . and those who find it are few."

A Sense of Direction

The way, simple and difficult though it may be, is to get a sense of direction and persistently to follow it.

This is the way.

There is no other.

No one else can do this for any of us, because it is an individual matter. For someone else to do it for us, if he could, would be our loss, for finding our way, becoming aware, is our great privilege. It can come "in the twinkling of an eye," when we are ready for it. Getting ready is what takes the time and effort.

We are in effect embarking on a journey, a journey back to the Father's house, a journey "from sense to soul." Allegorically this is true. In deepest truth it is not, for we are in the Father's house now—if only we truly know it. As Emmet Fox put it: "You will never be nearer to God through all eternity than you are right at this moment. As time passes you will realize it more, but you will not be nearer than you are right now. God will never love you more than He does right now." We are never separate from God—if only we know it. Separateness is an illusion of the senses. We are not separate from God nor from the forms of good we need to fulfill our sense of peace and purpose, nor are we even separate from one another.

A very simple illustration of apparent separateness and actual oneness may be found in the kind of pincushion that was popular in a less sophisticated age (when, incidentally, pins were not as abundant and inexpensive as they are now). Thrifty housewives often had pincushions in the shape and coloring, say, of an apple; in other words, spherical, or nearly so. They would thrust pins into the cushion until only the pin heads appeared on the surface.

The pin heads, if you can forgive the apparent disparagement, may be compared to ourselves as physical beings, the surface of the cushion to the surface of the earth. Looking only at the cushion and the bright little globs of metal, and seeing them only as they appear, it is obvious that they are all separate and apart. But all of us know that the little globs are the heads of pins that extend to the very center of the sphere of cotton, so that they touch one another at their points.

We are like that. To appearances we are all separate and apart. We may not even be aware that our being reaches to a center where we are one, or very close to one, with each other. But it is true.

We are very close to the truth of being when we realize, sense, believe what the three preceding paragraphs are trying to say.

We have started on a metaphorical journey. Unity is a form of faith that helps us to find our way. For Unity is a way of life.

This book is an endeavor to chart the way, so to speak. Perhaps no book can do more than this.

Basic Principles

Within the pages that follow you will find the basic principles of Unity's way of life. These do not constitute a final statement, for the statement of principles is subject to many forms of presentation. But though not final, they are fundamental. They have been tried, tested, proved by countless individuals. They have been presented in a great many Unity books, and in other books; but Unity's presentation reaches back to first-century Christianity, to the simple but often very challenging statements and works of the great Nazarene, and even to the works and teachings of other great teachers before Him.

They are an attempt to put the ageless truths of being into the vocabulary and frame of reference of present day mores.

If this book, then, serves any useful purpose it will not be simply a book to be read through at a sitting, or many sittings, and put on a shelf. It is rather a kind of book of instruction. Read it until you come to something to do. Then it is well to stop and try out for yourself what it suggests that you do. You may have to take it on faith, for the results of the doing, though they may start immediately, are not necessarily at once apparent.

It has in most cases taken us years to reach the particular states of mind, emotion, attitudes, that characterize us individually at the present time. But just as in the case of a man whose legs have been injured and restored, it may take a while for him to learn to walk again, so with this project. For Unity is not only a Truth to know, but a way to go. Let's start!

About God

How can a man know God?

"I've read scores of books about Him. I can quote long passages verbatim. I have the letter of it, but I don't have the spirit. I don't feel anything about Him," says a student.

Perhaps that word *feel* is the magic word. Feeling is the secret, when we endeavor to experience the deep things of the spiritual nature.

How shall we begin?

You have to begin where you are, and with what is familiar to you. You probably have to begin by thinking, and see where, if anywhere, your thinking leads you.

It is axiomatic that the place to begin anything is at the beginning. In mundane affairs this usually means to begin at the bottom, and to make progress we work up from there. In spiritual efforts we begin at the top; and here, too, we actually begin at the beginning, because God is the beginning. The very first words in the Bible are "In the beginning God . . . " But that is not where most of us begin our conscious thinking in trying to find our way out of the confusions that assail us. We usually begin with our troubles.

To begin with thoughts of disease, want, and misery and try to reconcile these with the thought of God is going at things the hard way. It is not an impossible way, for no matter where we are in thought God can reach us, and no matter where we are we can reach God. But there is a better way; and that way is to begin with God. Beginning with Him is like bringing light into darkness. And we might paraphrase St. Augustine's statement, "God is a circle whose center is everywhere and whose circumference is nowhere," saying instead, "God is a light whose center is everywhere and whose circumference is nowhere." Wisely we do not fight or resist the darkness; we bring in the light.

How do you think about God?

When you try to think about Him do you see a big Man sitting on a throne somewhere in the sky, surrounded by the four creatures and twenty-four elders? Or have you tried to comprehend what John meant when he said that "God is [a] spirit, and those who worship him must worship him in spirit and truth"?

Can you think of God in terms of attributes?

Suppose you try the thought, "God is life." That should be the easiest of all; it is free from dogmatic connotations. You see life all about you. Or do you? Do you really see life? Or would it be more accurate to say that you see the *expressions* of life? Animal, vegetable, mineral life. Life on land, life in the sea, life in the air; life that is obvious or animate, life that is not obvious and that we (hesitantly) describe as inanimate. Hesitantly, because even rock seems to have a kind of life of its own. It is a mass of pulsating atoms. Its interior structure is often amazingly beautiful. Seen through the eye of a microscope, its atoms are revealed to be in a state of frenetic but orderly activity. Or if you should be so fortunate as to break open just the right kind of boulder you might find its center to be hollow and lined with incredibly beautiful crystals of amethyst.

The Embodiment of Life

And what of you yourself? Are you not the veritable embodiment of life? You stand by the sea and waves come crashing toward you, dispersing into little ripples that reach toward your feet. You feel the ocean breeze caressing your face, your body. A gull's cry mingles with the sound of the waves. The winged form traces patterns in the air. The sun's rays beat down upon your upturned face. You feel your oneness with sea and sky and bird and air.

Whence came all these life forms, fluid, airy, solid, colorful, pulsing with a mysterious energy? Some call it a fortuitous conglomeration of atoms. Others call it God. But have you ever read a scientist's calculations of the fantastic chances against even one of these wonders having happened accidentally? (See Morrison's "Man Does Not Stand Alone," or Andrews' *The Symphony of Life*.)

Life! How do you explain it? You cannot. But you can feel it, you can respond to it, because you are a part of it. More than this; you are you. You are not a body, not even just a mind (either of which, body or mind, is to be regarded with the greatest reverence and awe). You are these, but you are more than these. You think, you feel, you move. You can activate your body. You can say to a hundred, nay, a thousand thoughts, "Go!" and they go, and occasionally a little less readily, "Come!" and they come. For you are more than flesh and bone and sinew, more even than thought and feeling. You are life-in-expression, a part of all the life there is. When you feel this, are you not aware of life? And is there a better name for it than God?

Or try thinking of God as love. What is love like? Have you ever seen it? What points in space does it occupy? How long? How wide? How deep? How much does it weigh? What are its colors? The story is told of a teacher who asked her little pupils to tell her what love is. They were mute. They squirmed in their places. They shook their heads. "Then tell me what love *does,*" she invited. One youngster came and put her arms around the teacher and kissed her. Another offered to clean the blackboard; a third, to empty the wastebasket.

We adults know that love has myriad forms, many faces. There are many aspects to its expression. It is more essential to our content and well-being than food or shelter or riches. We grow into an awareness of how important to our sense of well-being it is to love and be loved in return—or to love without thought of return—because it is in the nature of our being to love, as a lamp sheds its light because that is the nature of a lamp, or as the sun sheds its rays because that is the nature of the sun.

What makes this so? Did you or anyone in the whole wide world make it so? Does all the love of all the people in the world offer the totality of love? Do men create it, or do they simply respond to it because it is universal, supernal, infinite?

God as Father

Jesus most often spoke of God as Father. In one way this tells us something about Jesus' human father, Joseph. It also affirms something very special about us and our relationship to God. If God is our Father, then something of His nature abides in us, and though we may on occasion be erring sons, we are not rejected. In the very moment that we turn to Him we find that He is already with us—never more than a thought away. And as God is Spirit, we are then, by our divine inheritance, spiritual, and destined to manifest this, our true nature.

Indeed this concept has a very pertinent relationship to the evolvement of what is now known as Unity. The story is told elsewhere, but it merits acknowledgment here at least. Back in the 1880's Myrtle Fillmore, mother of three growing sons, was told by medical authorities that she had contracted tuberculosis (or as it was called in those days, consumption). And in those days the common thought was that this was inherited. She was given just six months to live. In desperation, she turned to the Scriptures. "If," as Jesus said, "God is our Father—and it is right there in Jesus' immortal prayer—then we can inherit only good from Him, and our inheritance from Him supercedes any human inheritance," was the gist of her thought.

The impact of this concept on her mind and emotions was emphatic, so much so that she rapidly regained physical strength and health. Neighbors were impressed. They asked for her prayers. "Better than praying for you, I will pray with you," was her response. A prayer group was formed. From this small beginning, a movement of simple Christian faith evolved.

Soon her husband, Charles Fillmore, who was crippled as the result of a childhood injury, became interested. Together they began to share their experience with small gatherings, by letter and the printed word. It was Charles Fillmore who described this ministry as Unity. "The word *Unity* appeared before my mind's eye in letters of gold," he said, describing the experience in some of his later writing.

In contemporary thought there are those who

reject the God-idea as being simply the outpicturing of man's need for a father-figure, someone who is authoritarian, and upon whom also we can blame our weaknesses and shortcomings.

But why should we feel such a need, why should we feel a sense of weakness or guilt or shortcoming, except that something within us calls us to a higher standard of thought, feeling and—to be very practical—performance? And we may find some comfort in the thought that if we can see our standards as being less than they should be, we have already reached past them in aspiration. What we can conceive, that we also can achieve.

Potentials

The father-concept may seem superficial to the casual thinker, as indicated in the introductory chapter. Viewed from the standpoint of Jesus, it is tremendous. It opens a whole new vista of potentials. It establishes a basic relationship whose possibilities are illimitable.

From this relationship all the other aspects of God evolve. If God is love, then we are "in love." We are in the love of God, and the love of God is in us. We are, by extension, loving.

Consider God as principle.

If God is Principle, then His action is all-pervading, includes us all, "shows no partiality." "God as principle is the absolute good expressed in all creation. When we know God and 'worship him in spirit and in truth' we recognize Him as this great goodness, which is omnipresent, omniscient, omnipotent, ready and willing to guide, to bless, and to uplift."

The apparent inequities and injustices of life are often a challenge to faith. We see, at its worst, the barbarity and bias of human laws and execution of justice that moved Dryden to exclaim, "Worth on foot, and rascals in the coach." Even at best, human efforts seem insufficient to make the ideal actual. Certainly we shall not be able to answer all human doubts and arguments in this paragraph or even in this book, but Peter points the direction in which we should turn our thought when he says, "Truly I perceive that God shows no partiality" (or in the more familiar King James version, "God is no respecter of persons"). And Peter no doubt got this conviction from Jesus, who said, according to Matthew, "Till heaven and earth pass away, not an iota, not a dot, will pass from the law until all is accomplished."

We do not always *see* it so, but then we do not always see the totality of the sequence from cause to effect. Often we see the cause and the effect so far separated by the passage of time as to obscure the precision of the law that Jesus was talking about.

The thought that God is principle, "with whom there is no variation or shadow due to change," may seem to be a very cold and impersonal concept; but by the same token it is our very present help, because it is absolutely dependable. If the laws of being (God) could be influenced by our human urgings, there would be no security. He might be *for* us one day, *against* us another. To know that He is always "for" the perfect action of justice requires only that we accord with what is right and best—that we be amenable, agreeable, to the action of divine law, and we are secure.

The sun shines. "He makes his sun rise on the evil and on the good, and sends rain on the just and the unjust." Men walk by its light. What they do of good or evil invites results that are forseeable to the man of understanding.

God as Substance

Somewhere in the Christian ethos the notion has evolved through the years that it is a kind of virtue to be poor, a sin to be prosperous. Emerson comments on this concept in his essay on "Compensation" when he says in part, "Was it that houses and lands, offices, wine, horses, dress, luxury, are had by unprincipled men, whilst the saints are poor and despised; and that a compensation is to be made to these last hereafter, by giving them the like gratification another day?" Timothy, in his first letter to Paul, writes, "As for the rich in this world, charge them not to be haughty, nor to set their hopes on uncertain riches but on God who richly furnishes us with everything to enjoy."

God promises us riches and honor, but also places a condition of fulfillment on every promise.

There is, so to speak, a "price on everything in life. You take what you want and pay for it," despite the assurance that "the best things in life are free." Free they may be of monetary considerations, but somehow or other we pay for them all, by giving them our time, our efforts, our attention, our appreciation, and perhaps most of all, our understanding. Without these, under grace and perfect law, everything we hold is at risk, but Jesus implied that it was very much a matter of putting first things first when He said, "Seek first his kingdom and his righteousness, and all these things shall be yours as well."

To have the matter put straight to us that God withholds from us no good thing, then, may come either as a shock or a relief. For every man must learn that use is the measure of possession. "Use or lose" is the law; but it is in the nature of God to provide us "enough and to spare," withholding nothing.

Charles Fillmore often discussed the nature of God as "substance," a concept seldom stressed outside New Thought. "What men need to know," he writes, "is that money represents a mind substance of unlimited abundance and accessibility; that this mind substance cannot safely be hoarded or selfishly used by anyone; that it is a living magnet attracting good of every kind to those who possess it."

Another writer declares: "Most of the great men of the Bible were either born prosperous, became prosperous or had access to riches whenever the need arose. Among them were Abraham, Jacob, Joseph, Moses, David, Solomon, Isaiah, Jeremiah, Nehemiah, Elijah, and Elisha of the Old Testament and Jesus and Paul of the New Testament."

Jesus wore the seamless robe, of such value that soldiers cast lots over who should possess it when it was taken from Him. He told His disciples how to acquire gold with which to pay taxes. He called forth loaves and fishes to appease the hunger of five thousand men on one occasion, four thousand on another, "besides women and children."

He appears to have been able to transmute the "invisible substance" of spiritual energy, as Charles Fillmore describes it, into whatever form answered the need of the moment, without being cumbered by "much possessions."

So we are coming to know something of "the mystery hidden for ages and generations but now made manifest to his saints. To them God chose to make known how great among the Gentiles are the riches of the glory of this mystery, which is Christ in you, the hope of glory."

Man

What is man that thou art mindful of him, and the son of man that thou dost care for him? Yet thou hast made him little less than God, and dost crown him with glory and honor—Psalms 8:4-6.

God made man upright, but they have sought out many devices—Eccles. 7:29.

God said, "Let us make man in our image, after our likeness" . . . then the Lord God formed man of the dust from the ground, and breathed into his nostrils the breath of life; and man became a living being—Gen. 1:26, 2:7.

When Moses wrote of the creation he wasted no words, covering eons in a few sentences. His history of primitive man is equally concise, though neither account is at odds with modern science.

Some readers of Genesis have thought that Moses must have been confused in his account of creation; that he repeated himself contradictorily and even shamefully, or that the two accounts as presented in the first and second chapters of Genesis are by different writers. Actually, however, a careful reading of the two chapters suggests that they portray two distinct steps in the order of creation.

The first step is in the realm of ideas. It is the thinking-out process, in which God dreams His plan for the creation of the heavenly bodies, of earth and sky and sea, and man. The account is a veritable poem, reaching a climax in the words, "let us make man in our image, after our likeness; and let them have dominion over the fish of the sea, and over the birds of the air, and over the cattle, and over all the earth, and over every creeping thing that creepeth upon the earth. So God created man in his own image, in the image of God he created him; male and female he created them."

God even planned what man's food should be, and seems to have intended him to be a vegetarian, for He said, "I have given you every plant yielding seed . . . and every tree with seed in its fruit; you shall have them for food."

This account comprises all of Chapter One in Genesis, and the first three verses of Chapter Two. In verses four and five we find this clarifying statement: "These are the generations of the heavens and of the earth . . . when no plant of the field was yet in the earth . . . and there was no man to till the ground." Then begins the appearance of what God had already created in mind: "But a mist went up from the earth and watered the whole face of the ground."

The first account describes God's conception of the universe and man; the second is devoted to the actual outpicturing of what He had been envisioning.

The Outpicturing

What Moses so briefly describes in these early chapters of Genesis is very much like some of the modern-day theories of creation. Science assumes a great power (which Moses called God), depicts the action of that power as motion ("and the Spirit of God was moving over the face of the waters"), generating light in the vastnesses of space ("and God said, Let there be light"), the condensation of moisture on the cooling earth, and the appearance of oceans and land ("Let the waters . . . be gathered together . . . and let the dry land appear"), and the evolutionary processes of life ("Let the earth put forth vegetation . . . Let the waters bring forth swarms of living creatures and let birds fly over the earth . . . And God made the beasts of the earth").

The climax of the manifest creation is reached in the passage, "Then the Lord God formed man of dust of the ground, and breathed into his nostrils the breath of life; and man became a living being."

Take a deep breath as you consider this statement. Note with what meticulous care the words are chosen. God had already *created* man "in his image, after his likeness," or in His divine imagination, and of like substance as Himself; that is, as a spiritual being. Now God *forms* man of the *dust of the ground!* What stupendous events are signalized in these few dramatic words!

What tremendous days were those six days or cycles of creativity by which life was quickened in the prehistoric seas of the cooling earth, and took the form of algae and amoeba, and gradually more and more complex and varied forms—forms that crept out upon the land; some of them—such as whales and giant turtles—only to return to their mother seas, others changing scales into feathers and flippers to wings and soaring into the air; still others making their home on the land, and evolving through countless species. Until finally, possibly in several separated places upon the earth, a creature appeared, truly formed from the "dust" of myriad forms that preceded it, into which God could breathe His mighty breath of life, so that "man became a living being."

Through how many eons of time, how many days

that are as a thousand years, had the spirit of God awaited that climactic moment! And how many more days of a thousand thousand years must it be before the "first man Adam" shall discover and apply himself to gaining his promised dominion! By now he has indeed conquered the so-called "lower" creations of the world around him, while yet needing to understand and master the world within himself. Then shall he become manifestly "the last for which the first was made"—the Christ man!

The Fall of Man

"The fall of man," which describes his eviction from the Garden of Eden, may yet be understood to mean his descent from the spiritual into the material world. Man himself has so named the world, and whatsoever he shall name it, that it shall be—to him. And thus he who was created to have dominion over all the things of the heavens and the earth has often become slave to them instead of their master, because he is not yet his own master.

Man is to learn that the spiritual and the material are actually not different in essence, but only in manifestation; that you might say (crudely but perhaps graphically) that matter is spirit condensed, and spirit is matter attenuated. Yet both are what Emerson called "one common stuff," in different rates and modes of motion or vibration.

That the two shall be reconciled in one body, as Paul said, is the challenge, the dilemma, and the opportunity of man. He is to achieve this reconciliation by means of soul or mind, the great conciliator. For manifest man is a threefold being, body, soul, and spirit, though essentially a spiritual being, born of the great creative Forces of being, or God. Thus, he *is* a spiritual being. He *has* a body. He *has* a soul. "Beloved, we are God's children now; it does not yet appear what we shall be, but we know that when he appears, we shall be like him, for we shall see him as he is."

In Charles Fillmore's words: "Man is spirit, soul, and body. . . . Soul is the sum total of man's experiences gathered throughout the ages. Soul has its inner and outer avenues of expression." Its inner expression is in what is usually described as the subconscious, the feeling nature: its outer expression is as intellect, the conscious mind that accepts, rejects, classifies, and names the things and circumstances of his present-life experiences, and whatever he names them, "good, bad, indifferent," that becomes their name *to him.*

Man's physical body is an approximation of the true spiritual body, which is whole, entire, perfect, "for . . . we have a house not made with hands, eternal in the heavens." In the mundane sense, the body is endowed with the physical characteristics of its progenitors, but it takes on more and more the aspects of the entity that dwells in it, until in maturity it becomes the embodiment of the thoughts, feelings, and attitudes of the person who animates it.

"Man's true business is the 'express' business," one writer has put it. For it is one thing to know *about* these things, and quite another to *act* with wisdom and understanding upon the things we know. As Jesus was to say, "If you know these things, blessed are you if you do them," and when before Pilate, He said, "For this was I born, and for this have I come into the world, to bear witness to the truth," He was not speaking of Himself alone, but of all men. "He who believes in me will also do the works that I do; and greater works than these will he do."

Original Sin?

Somewhere in the remote past the assertion was made that man was "conceived in sin and brought forth in iniquity." Perhaps because mankind is all too aware that in the matter of the propagation of the species as in many other things he often falls short of his own ideals of motivation and behavior, he has been willing, even eager, to excuse himself on the basis of "original sin." The theologians have emphasized this concept down through the centuries, and the acceptance of this view of himself has impressed upon man a deep sense of guilt. To free himself from this sense of guilt, of innate sin and depravity, and like the prodigal in the parable to return again home—to the sense of his oneness with his Father God—is man's great spiritual emprise.

There is a fascinating sidelight on this expression, "conceived in sin and brought forth in iniquity," that does not alter what it is that man has yet to do, but offers an interesting (if somewhat whimsical) interpretation of the assertion. In mythology, in astrology, in Biblical symbology, twelve is the number of fulfillment, completion: twelve signs of the zodiac, twelve labors of Hercules, twelve half-tones in the octave of music, twelve months of the year, twelve sons of Jacob, twelve tribes of Israel, twelve faculties of mind, twelve apostles of Jesus and of Buddha.

From the conception to the birth of the human child is normally nine months. This period of conception "falls short" of the round of twelve. One of the meanings of "sin" is "to fall short" (of the mark, as in archery). The word *sin* is cognate with the Hebrew words *Sin* and *Shin,* next to the last letter (*Tav*) of the Hebrew alphabet (again, the suggestion of "falling short of the mark" of completion). The words *iniquity* and *inequity* relate to imbalance, inequality, and by intimation "falling short" of perfection or fulfillment. So man must be "born again" to complete the round or cycle.

But these are man's assertions, based on his own limited evaluation of his own origin and nature. In the sight of God, in ultimate truth, man is truly the son of God, heir to all he surveys, capable of infinite possibilities, limited only by his own lack of spiritual awareness. In his progress from sense to spirit, he is often dominated by the obvious rather than the real, and must patiently and persistently seek to follow the intimations from the God-nature within him that he is more than flesh and blood, more even than mind and spirit, thereby regain his lost dominion, and become in fact what he is and always has been in truth: a spiritual being, full of grace and truth.

Thinking

"I am the Lord of my mentality, and the ruler of my thought people," asserts Charles Fillmore. Your mind is your kingdom. Your thoughts are your subjects. Mind can make men giants of capability, or can dwarf all their accomplishments. When you rule your thoughts you rule your world. If you do not like the world as you see it, you can transform it "more nearly to the heart's desire" by changing your thoughts about yourself and it.

When we read in Genesis that the Lord said to Abram, "the land which you see I will give to you," we "see" (that is, we "understand") that this applies not only to what Abram saw with his eyes but what he saw with his mind. A similar point is made in the story of Jacob, who placed spotted sticks in the watering troughs where plain-colored animals, heavy with young, came to drink. Seeing spots they thought spots, thinking spots they conceived spots, conceiving spots they brought forth spots, so that their young were "striped, speckled, and spotted." That in the view of modern medical knowledge such a result seems extremely unlikely only serves to make the mental parallel of the story the more emphatic; in short that—

What you see in your mind's eye, that you will think,

What you think, that you will conceive,

What you conceive, that you will bring forth.

When you choose your thought you choose

results. Even when you think at random, you are still unconsciously choosing results—haphazard results. For everything brings forth after its kind, as the account in Genesis so forcefully reminds us. This is the fundamental law of manifestation: "First the blade, then the ear, then the full grain in the ear." Thought, then, is formative, and in obedience to the law of manifestation whatever we picture in our mind as thought, we tend to bring forth in experience. Shakespeare voices this concept through Hamlet, when he says, "There is nothing either good or bad, but thinking makes it so."

Man's thoughts are both his strength and his weakness; strength when he understands this law and applies himself to it; weakness when he allows himself to be dominated by appearances, by the way things look. In such a state of mind, he is no longer the initiator of events, but only a re-acter.

It usually seems to us that we are subject to and dominated by forces outside ourselves. "It is not the circumstances of your life that are most important, but rather your attitude toward them; how you permit them to affect you."

Thoughts Change People

Change your thoughts and, in effect, you change everything; that is, you change your relationship to environment, and your evaluation of environment. You consciously choose, out of all possible reactions, which ones you will permit to influence your thinking, and how. This is the significance of the admonition, "You will only look with your eyes, and see the recompense of the wicked." "With your eyes" . . . in other words, you will not allow the sight of negative and destructive situations to get past your eyes into your strong thoughts and deep feelings where they can do you unnecessary harm, and do no one else any good.

"Do not be overcome by evil, but overcome evil with good," Paul wrote to the Romans. Nothing can overcome you but your belief in your own weakness and futility. Nothing can make you strong but the discovery of your own strength and adequacy. Elephants might have become the rulers of the world if brute strength were the ultimate power; but man, physically weak by comparison, has become their master by reason of his mind; by the power of thought.

So, "do not be deceived; God is not mocked, for whatever a man sows, that he will also reap." For "they sow the wind, and they shall reap the whirlwind," which is another way of saying, "What you send out shall come back to you increased and multiplied." This is the nature of thought.

"There is but one Mind in the entire universe, and this Mind is God," writes Dr. H. Emilie Cady. "Why does He not keep our thoughts right instead of permitting us through ignorance to drift into wrong thoughts, and so bring trouble on ourselves?

"Well, we are not automatons. Your child will never learn to walk alone if you always do his walking. Because you recognize that the only way for him to be strong, self-reliant in all things—in other words, to become a man—is to throw him on himself, and let him, through experience, come to a knowledge of things for himself, you are not willing to make a mere puppet of him by taking the steps for him, even though you know that he will fall down many times and give himself severe bumps in his ongoing toward perfect physical manhood." And we might add that it's not being down that counts, but getting up and going on.

So long as man continues to form mental concepts at variance with the inner urge of the soul for good, just so long will he remain a house divided against itself. The thoughts of our mind and the feelings of our heart are responsible for what appears in our world, even though it does not seem to be so. Paul tells us that "by faith we understand that the world was created by the word of God, so that what is seen was made out of things which do not appear." *Things which are seen are not made of things that do appear.* Thoughts and feelings on the one hand and manifestation on the other are seed and fruit of the same plant. To change the one we must change the other.

If you want to change the pictures that appear on a motion picture screen you do not slash the screen or turn off the light. You change the film in the projector.

Thought is Formative

The nature of thought is formative. The evidence is everywhere, and we can trace both its baleful and its beneficent effects all about us. Indeed we ourselves are the embodied evidence of this fact.

We receive a promotion, the visit of a friend, a delightful gift, and the message of happiness is sent along all the nerve "wires" of the body. We feel a definite, buoyant physical reaction; the blood circulates more energetically, and the increased energy demands expression. We laugh, we dance, we jump up and down, we whistle or sing, or in some other manner we give evidence of the vitalizing influence of the experience. The mind, too, is favorably affected and the initial impulse activates new ideas, mental pictures, plans, projects.

Contrariwise, what havoc bad news can play with our mind, body, and activities. We feel depressed, have difficulty in holding to a definite sequence of thought, the blood flows sluggishly, the appetite fails, we become weak and discouraged.

Charles Fillmore puts it like this: "Thought is the creative power by which man builds mentality and a body of perfection. Man understandingly uses his creative thought power by mentally perceiving the right relation of ideas; 'what he seeth the Father doing,' as stated by Jesus. Thus we see the necessity not only for thinking right thoughts, but also for having a right basis for our thinking. We must think according to universal Principle. The successful mathematician bases all his calculations on the rules of mathematical science; so the successful metaphysician bases his creative thinking on the unlimited ideas of the one Mind."

"Life," he asserts, "in Divine Mind is unlimited as an *idea* back of perpetual, omnipresent action, but by man's thought it may be subjected to many limitations . . . All ideas have their foundation in Divine Mind, but man has put the limitation of his negative thought upon them, and sees them 'in a mirror, darkly.'

"Applying this reasoning to individual consciousness, we find just how man thinks his body into disease."

Thought tends to carry over into form, so that a person tends to take on the lineaments of what he thinks. To know what a man thinks, observe what he says and does, how he feels about things. He is, in his maturity, the embodiment of what he habitually thinks.

And if, indeed, we find how a man thinks his body into disease, we may also find how a man may think his body out of disease and into health.

"Begin now to speak words of strength and health—and keep it up. Do not look at what has been. Lot's wife tried that, and she never got beyond the past . . . The thought makes the body and determines the condition it lives in."

Self-Defeating?

Sometimes our concern about constructive thinking can defeat or at least deter the results we desire. Fear of evil is not the same thing as love of the good, nor is anxiety about wrong thinking the same as thinking right. "My zeal consumes me," cried the Psalmist, and again, "zeal for thy house has consumed me." Jesus cautioned the disciples in a similar vein in His discourse on anxiety, quoted in Matthew. "Which of you by being anxious can add one cubit to his span of life?" He asks. No, anxiety only defeats its purpose. When will and imagination come into conflict, imagination wins. When aspiration and conviction are at odds, a man will be ruled by his convictions. Thought is most effective when it is accompanied by deep feeling; "As he thinketh in his heart, so is he," is the familiar version, and "Keep your heart with all vigilance; for from it flow the springs of life." Feeling is the secret.

If you are aware of entertaining a negative or destructive thought, let it be like a spark falling on your coat sleeve. Let the spark remain, and it may burn a hole on the fabric. Brush it off, and it will do no damage. Forget it and go on. So with thoughts. It is very difficult in a relative world to be one hundred percent right, or for that matter, one hundred percent wrong. Set your vision on a goal of attainment, point your efforts in the right direction, and you will make continual and rewarding progress.

For the most part we are not too aware of the tenor of our habitual thoughts. When someone who knows us very well calls our attention to some habitual turn of speech that we employ, it may come to us as a great surprise, just as when someone plays back a tape-recording of something we have said. "Why, I don't sound like that!" is a commonplace reaction. So it becomes obvious to us that to change our use of the powers of mind that are potentially ours requires what amounts to re-education. It is like learning to play piano by note when we have been playing by ear. Perhaps we played quite acceptably, though with limited variation, until we tried to change to playing by note. For a time we could do neither one very well; but the ultimate gain could be mastery of the keyboard—well worth persistent effort and dedication. It is so with the power of deeply-felt thought.

Thinking constructively produces constructive results. Emerson says, "the dice of God are always loaded," which seems an astonishing thing to say of God. Yet Emerson's wisdom is apparent, for the power of God always favors the good, the better, the best. In the beginning He pronounced all that He had made to be "very good." We should do no less.

Reality is Enduring

All that is real in any experience is the good. The evil in things exists, but in a transient and relative sense, rather than an absolute sense. It is good out of place, or misdirected. That is, the evil exists in our consciousness or understanding, in our point of view. In the absolute or eternal sense, it has no reality. For to be real, a thing must be eternal. Evil is to goodness as darkness is to light. "Once you were in darkness, but now you are light in the Lord; walk as children of light," admonished the Master Jesus.

"Every man who accomplishes things sees first in his mind what he wishes to do. He puts away all doubt. It makes no difference how small or how large the thing you want to do may be; if you have an unlimited confidence in your ability to do it, you will do it. Nothing can in any way impede or defeat you," wrote Charles Fillmore. "You can cultivate the habit of seeing the good, the true, the bright side of every subject, and when with your friends you can bring this side out in conversation, thus keeping yourself positive and poised, and at the same time sowing the seed of Truth in the minds of others."

Control your thought and you dominate circumstances.

To become free from the domination of the shadow of evil, it is necessary to become increasingly conscious of the light of goodness.

The acceptance of evil places us under its law. To call forth the good in our life, we must "agree" with the good, we must direct our attention toward the good; "hug it to our heart," give it our enthusiasm, animate it by our imagination. We must become so thoroughly imbued with the consciousness of good that evil ceases to exist for us—"ceases to exist" in the sense that we no longer give it the power of our strong thought and deep feeling, recognizing it only for what it is, a temporal appearance, a shadow, a picture on a screen.

The commandment that Moses received from God, "You shall not bear false witness," is in consonance with this principle of agreement. False witness is testimony to or acknowledgment of that which is false—the appearance of evil. Paul's admonition to the church at Rome confirms this viewpoint: "Be not overcome of evil, but overcome evil with good." Let us not, then, bear witness to evil, but let our life testify to our faith in the dominance of good, so that we can say with Joshua, "as for me and my house, we will serve the Lord."

Appearances

Regardless of what appears to be true, our constant privilege and opportunity is to bear witness to the Truth, to be true witnesses; to behold, testify to, and proclaim the good. If we look upon anything and behold evil, then we must look deeper; deep enough and spiritually enough to see truly. We must look until we can find a point of agreement with the principle of good.

"My body is the servant of my mind, and my mind is the servant of God," affirms Charles Fillmore. In this he is approaching one of the trinities, such as mind, idea, and expression, that characterizes everything in this world of manifestation. The blade, the ear, the full grain in the ear; father, mother, and child; ice, water, steam; body, mind, and God-mind; spirit, soul, and body: and thus we come to the consideration of three ways in which mind manifests for us individually.

The conscious mind is the one with which we are most familiar. Another term for it is the intellect, or the thinking faculty. It is the phase of mind that thinks things out consciously; that chooses courses of action; makes decisions, gives orders.

The subconscious mind is the storehouse of

memory, the feeling nature. It does not give orders, but faithfully carries out instructions from the conscious mind.

The Superconscious Mind is the God-mind, the overshadowing presence of the emerging Christ nature in man.

One writer has said: "You may liken the body to a business organization with three partners in charge: The Number One Man (superconsciousness) is the Idea Man, who knows all the principles and methods for successful operation, but does not force ideas on the Number Two Man (consciousness), the manager, who gives all the orders to the Number Three man (subconsciousness), the production department. Number Three Man is completely obedient, does not evaluate the orders, simply produces what is called for in the orders. Successful operation is guaranteed if Number Two Man will always consult with Number One Man before making decisions and giving orders. Difficulty arises when Number Two Man is indifferent to or ignorant of his ability to contact Number One Man."

There is only one Mind, the Mind of God. It is the First Cause, from which all else emerges. What we call our mind is the use we make of the Mind of God manifesting in us. "The life of man is a self-evolving circle, which, from a ring imperceptibly small, rushes on all sides outwards to new and larger circles, and that without end. . . . There is no outside, no enclosing wall, no circumference to us." We might paraphrase this by saying that God is a light whose center is everywhere and whose circumference is nowhere. From the center of light within us we reach in thought to the center of Being, where we are unified with infinite Mind, Light, and Love, so that we radiate light and love to all the world, fulfilling the admonition of that embodiment of light and love who said: "I am the light of the world." "You are the light of the world." "Walk as children of light."

Truth

"Truth is within ourselves; it takes no rise
From outward things, whate'er you may believe.
There is an inmost center in us all
Where truth abides in fullness; and around,
Wall upon wall, the gross flesh hems it in,
This perfect, clear perception—which is truth.
A baffling and perverting carnal mesh
Binds it, and makes all error; and to know
Rather consists in opening out a way
Than in effecting entry for a light
Supposed to be without."

—Browning

"Truth . . . is the intuitive perception of what is right in the sight of God."—Charles Fillmore.

What determines the human condition? Are the events of our life, our health or illness, our wealth or poverty, our veritable human relationship to others determined by chance? If so, it would seem that there is nothing to be done but make the best of things. But we look at the world around us, and we observe that in ages past people thought that everything was governed by chance, or by capricious and unpredictable deities who must be bribed or cajoled, or if offended—and human misfortunes were attributed to such offenses—must be appeased by sacrifices.

Some people still so believe. But mostly people now recognize that there are universal laws—laws that make the positions and movements of the stars and planets predictable for centuries to come; laws of electricity, of gravity, of motion and inertia; laws that are applicable to the human body in which we dwell, that govern circulation of the blood, the response of the nerves to stimuli, and that mysteriously transform the food and drink we imbibe into tissue and bone and blood.

If all this and more, a thousand times ten thousand more, is true of the world about us, of the body in which we dwell, are we, "the person in the body," exempt? We see evidences of a grand design in the universe which suggest an overruling supreme Intelligence. To entertain such a concept is difficult perhaps for us but it is easier to do so than to estimate the incomprehensible chances against so elaborate and intelligent an organization of matter and forces having come about by mere chance; as if a hundred monkeys at a hundred typewriters and no knowledge of English would eventually produce the text of Shakespeare's "Hamlet" (as someone has suggested).

Are the known laws of nature, of physics, of mathematics, ever overthrown? Arguments are so very much against it that if there is an appearance of such an exception, we would have to believe that we misread it, or else deduce that the action of some other law as yet unknown to us had produced the apparent contradiction.

What, then, of man? If it were the plan and purpose of such an Intelligence that man should be ignorant, afflicted, impoverished, miserable, would there be any reasonable hope of betterment? And if there is such a hope, is not this hope itself the evidence that these limitations are not a part of such a plan and purpose?

If we experience these negative *facts* of our human existence, are they the *Truth?* If not, then what *is* the Truth?

Man's Discontent

There is one "fact" that suggests a purpose and a principle; that fact is that universally mankind seeks betterment. We are not content with illness, poverty, imperfection, or even our own transient concepts of perfection. "There must be something better than this" is man's declaration, and his pursuit of this often vague intimation is the starting point that leads to his growing conviction–perhaps *awareness* is a better word–that back of changing facts there is changeless principle; principle which is the ultimate overcoming and fulfillment of his efforts at attaining health of body, serenity of mind, tranquillity of spirit. It leads him to identify not primarily with the transient but with the eternal, not with the illusory, but with the real; less with fact, more with principle.

This can lead him to the concept that if it were God's intention that he be weak, sick, miserable, unhappy, all efforts at change would be unavailing. That these things can be and are being changed implies that "nothing is ever settled until it is settled right," and that as Paul wrote to the Corinthians, "our knowledge is imperfect, and our prophecy is imperfect; but when the perfect comes [to individual consciousness?] the imperfect will pass away." "Pass away," truly, but since we are manifesting in a realm of time, or progressive change, usually it will pass away gradually. Gradually, because the Truth seems to human reasoning too good to be true!

What is the truth of our being? Can man transcend the Infinite? Is man's own imagination better than that of his Creator? Is not man's own highest dream but an approximation of the Truth? "We are God's children now; it does not yet appear what we shall be" declared one of great insight.

Truth, as we apply the term in metaphysics, is the ultimate reality back of all creation; the fullness and completeness of what we experience partially and sequentially in this mundane world of time, space, and form. We often make "corrections" of what appears to be true from where we are in this earthly realm to come closer to what is even true in the relative and mundane sense. We observe a train disappearing on the rails. Observation is that the rails converge, the train shrinks in size. Experience affirms the correction.

The Pattern is Constant

We refer to our physical body as if it were a constant, yet we know that it is composed of myriad tiny bodies, and that in a short period of time, a few years, all the elements that compose it are completely replaced, so that in a quite literal physical sense, it is not the same body. The pattern is the same; the constituents change.

When we say "body," do we mean the body as it is at the moment of speaking; as it was five, ten, twenty years ago; or as it will be in years to come? Perhaps we mean all of these: what in some Oriental theology is termed "the long body," the body from birth to death. Does all of this put together describe the Truth about the body? "Every person," Charles Fillmore declares, "has a perfect body in mind, and that perfect body . . . is bringing itself into manifestation just as fast as he (the person in the body) will let it."

To repeat: "Our knowledge is imperfect, and our

prophecy is imperfect; but when the perfect comes, the imperfect will pass away." Truly when that which is perfect, entire, complete shall come in our understanding, that which is imperfect will no longer be a part of our consciousness—will "pass away."

When you have mastered the principle of anything, you are no longer in bondage to previously held mistaken concepts. "You will know the truth, and the truth will make you free." Our degree of freedom in any area of life is commensurate with our degree of understanding of the principles involved, and our right relationship to them.

The English author Arthur Christopher Benson symbolically portrays freedom and bondage in his imaginative novel, "Child of the Dawn." In one episode he is escorted by his guide, Amroth, into an awesome institution-like building. They enter a corridor from which he can see into adjacent rooms as if looking through prison bars, at the occupants who are unaware of being observed. He sees what appears to be a charming study. There are book-lined walls, a desk, a green-shaded reading lamp. A man rises from his desk chair and begins pacing the floor as if lost in thought. Amroth says in effect: "Here is a well-meaning man who has become so enrapt in philosophy and metaphysics that he has lost the common touch. He has shut out the people and problems of the world, shut out even his own wife and children. He is in self-imposed imprisonment. But see, he is becoming restless. He is beginning to miss his home, his family. Soon he will think and love his way into freedom."

"That which we pronounce truth from the plane of appearances is relative only. The relative truth is constantly changing, but the absolute truth endures;

and what is true today always was and always will be true," says Charles Fillmore.

Everything that was ever real and true is no less real and true in the face of apparent contradictions. Adverse appearances cannot change eternal verities: the underlying principles of life are constant. The laws of mathematics are not altered because someone gets a wrong answer to a problem. The law of action and reaction is not abrogated because we do not see it in its true accord. The stars still "come nightly to the sky" and the heavens still "declare the glory of God" when clouds obstruct the view of them.

Every access of knowledge opens doorways of understanding.

Are you disparaging of the religious customs of faiths that differ from your own? A Protestant chaplain in World War II found that his prayers for Catholic and Jewish soldiers dying on the battlefields meant nothing to them, gave them no comfort. Wisely he sought out a Catholic chaplain who familiarized him with the appropriate prayers. He got a Jewish rabbi to write out in phonetic form the Hebraic prayers for the dying. Finally when he achieved the rank of colonel he was able to get the prayers for these and related uses printed in pamphlet form for the use of other chaplains like himself.

Respect Replaces Fear

Men used to fear the lightning; but one man faced that age-old fear, and found out how to harness the lightning to constructive uses for all mankind.

Men feared the uncharted spaces of the seas until one brave soul set out to face that fear, and found a new world. The oceans that were barriers to intercourse between continents became highways of intercourse and commerce.

Men feared the skies. They pictured witches on broomsticks, hobgoblins, demons in the air. Some even pictured an anthropomorphic God "out there." Intrepid fliers and inventive scientists working together have banished these fearful fancies. And those who do not believe in God at all cited their negative report as confirmation of their unbelief.

The most enduring and most precious things in life, contrary to mundane man's usual sense of values, are not in the realm of the manifest, the realm of things that can be sensorily perceived, that can be weighed, measured, seen, felt, touched, embraced. Yet even the man whose extrasensory perceptivity is most limited finds many of his satisfactions in the realm of the intangible. Does he not love? Does he not long to be loved, and find joy in the experience?

Yet what point in space does love occupy? What are its dimensions, how much does it weigh? Can you possess it, put it in a container for safekeeping? Is it less real for all this? Is it not more real, more vital, than any form of life through which it manifests? Does it not, to our amazement, have a meaning apart from our employment of its virtues?

"In reality," says Ouspensky, in his book "Tertium Organum," "love is a cosmic phenomenon, in which men, humanity, are merely accidents; a cosmic phenomenon which has nothing to do with either the lives or the souls of men, any more than because the sun is shining, by its light men may go about their little affairs, and may utilize it for their own purposes." So it is with Truth. So it is with wisdom. So it is when we are considering principle.

Truth cannot be communicated; it must be

evolved. It must be experienced. We may know about it, but we cannot really know it until we experience it. It may seem harsh, cold, relentless. Even worse, it may seem vague or nonexistent, until in some human predicament, searching for answers on the mundane level and finding none, our importunity becomes God's opportunity, and the cold, impersonal, unfeeling is warmed by our heart's need, and "comes alive" in our consciousness! Alive to the concept that we are the sons of God.

As a son of God, what are your characteristics?

As a son of God, you are endowed with infinite possibilities. You are essentially a spiritual being. You have within you the all-creating powers of the Most High. You can do all things needful. You can overcome all the limitations that in your mundane, physical, human nature you seem heir to. Your inheritance from your Creator takes precedence over any earthly, human, or mundane inheritance. You are not subject to injustice or condemnation. You attract your own as by divine right. Nothing and no one can keep from you or take from you that which by reason of your divine nature and origin is rightfully yours. You claim your good and press your claim. You do not combat evil or negation. You recognize that they have no more power than human thought, feeling, and acceptance give them. In the light of Truth they are dispelled as mists before the morning sun.

Jesus Christ

"John sent two of his disciples to Jesus to ask if He were the Christ; 'Then Jesus answering said unto them, Go your way and tell John what things ye have seen and heard.' It was the pragmatic test to which He appealed, how His religion worked, the severest and the certainest test in the world. Christianity, insofar as it is truly Christian, rests upon the same solid foundations as chemistry."–Edwin E. Slosson, "Sermons of a Chemist."

Jesus Christ is both the Way-Shower and the Way: Way-Shower in His nature as Jesus, the Son of man; Way in His nature as Christ, the Son of God. Of those who know about Him, some accept the Man but fail to do anything about His message, others accept the message but even doubt the Messenger's existence. Still others see the two, the Man and the message, the Way-Shower and the Way as inseparably united.

Some say that to make Jesus the center of worship is taking "a crystallized and stereotyped backward glance into the time of Jesus" but that "Christianity should glance at the life and times of Jesus 2,000 years ago, but a *look forward* to the Christ Spirit in all men and the expectancy of its fulfillment. Did He not say 'You, therefore, must be perfect, as your heavenly Father is perfect'?"

It was perhaps out of some such need that the word picture entitled "One Solitary Life" was written. It is attributed to a minister, The Rev. George

Clarke Peck.

"More than nineteen hundred years ago there was born a man who lived in poverty and was reared in obscurity, the child of a peasant woman.

"In infancy He startled a king. In childhood He puzzled doctors. He worked in a carpenter's shop until He was thirty, then for three years He was an itinerant preacher. In manhood He ruled the course of nature—He walked upon the waves as if they were pavement, and hushed the sea to sleep.

"He never wrote a book. Never held an office. Never owned a home. Never had a family. Never went to college. Never put His foot inside a big city. Never traveled two hundred miles from the place where He was born. He never did one of the things that accompany greatness. He possessed neither wealth or influence. He had no credentials but Himself.

"While still a young man, the tide of public opinion turned against Him. His friends ran away. He was turned over to His enemies. He went through the mockery of a trial. He was nailed to a cross between two thieves. While He was dying, His executioners gambled for the only piece of property He had on earth—His coat. When He was dead, He was laid in a borrowed grave through the pity of a friend.

"He never marshaled an army, or drafted a soldier, or fired a gun; and yet no other leaders ever had more volunteers, who have, under His orders, persuaded more rebels to stack arms and surrender without a shot being fired.

"Every seventh day the wheels of commerce cease their turning and multitudes wend their way to worship assemblies to pay homage and respect to Him. Nineteen centuries have come and gone, and today

He is the central figure of the human race and the leader of the column of progress.

"I am far in the mark when I say that all the armies that ever marched, and all the navies that ever sailed, and all the parliaments that ever sat, and all the kings that ever reigned, put together, have not affected the life of man upon this earth as has that *one solitary life!*

"Herod could not destroy Him. The grave could not hold Him. He stands forth upon the highest pinnacle of glory; proclaimed of God, acknowledged by angels, adored by saints, and feared by devils as the living personal Christ, our Lord and Savior.

"Because of His life, death, and resurrection we have the hope, the assurance of eternal life."

The Pattern Life

In a similar way the "backward glance" at the time and toward the person of Jesus the Christ can serve a great purpose for the aspiring soul who would become a "follower of the Way." It will not only reveal aspects of the teaching that might not otherwise have been clear, but it will acquaint you with the wise and loving nature of One who not only taught the Truth but who lived it.

Most of us are in this respect somewhat like the little boy who was tucked into his bed in his darkened room, and who made repeated excuses to get attention and company.

"Now, Sonnie, just close your eyes and go to sleep. Remember, God is with you."

"Yes, I know. But I want a god with skin on!" was the boy's response.

And so do we all. We not only want the statement of the Truth. We long for the evidence of it.

Have you ever climbed a long hill or a mountain ("because it was there!") and found that after what seemed interminable effort the way ahead looked almost as long and as hard as when you started? If so, look back and see how far you have come. It will reassure you and give you courage to keep going.

Or have you perhaps allowed yourself to become overwhelmed by the reports of violence in the cities, wars among nations, the pollution of the earth's natural resources, and a host of other problems that you read in the daily press, hear on the radio, see on television? If so, you may be moved to echo the words of Isaiah, "How beautiful upon the mountains are the feet of him who brings good tidings, who publishes peace."

Viewing the teachings of Jesus, no matter how true, apart from His own vibrant, warm, and loving personality, they are still cold and abstract. In Him they come alive, and what comes from the heart of One who so deeply lived the Truth warms our own hearts, and strengthens the desire to fulfill His admonition, "If you know these things, blessed are you if you do them." "The words that I say to you I do not speak on my own authority; but the Father who dwells in me does his works. Believe me that I am in the Father and the Father in me; or else believe me for the sake of the works themselves . . . he who believes in me will also do the works that I do; and greater works than these will he do." The next words, often taken to refer to His approaching death, actually reveal instead the way by which the works are done: "because I go to the Father." This He did continually, and admonished others to do.

The Way would be more difficult for most of us without the Way-Shower, for in Him we find the embodiment of what all men truly are and are to be. For though to human sense we are sons of earth, eternally we are sons of God and heaven.

Name and Title

Jesus, then, is the name of the strong Man of Galilee, who in His human aspect so often referred to Himself as the Son of man. Christ is not the name of a person, but is a title representing the divine nature of God in man. From the Greek word *Christos,* it has much the same significance as the Hebrew word *Messiah.* It is clearly used in this sense in Matthew 16:13 *et seq* when Jesus asks the disciples, "Who do men say that the Son of man is?"

They answer Him in a manner that indicates the kind of speculation about successive human embodiments, reincarnation, that was common at the time (and is having a renascence in the present as well).

"Some say John the Baptist [come to life again], others say Elijah, and others Jeremiah or one of the prophets."

Jesus pressed the point. "But who do you say that I am?"

Peter, reaching past conjectures concerning Jesus' pre-existence, responded, "You are the Christ, the Son of the living God!"

And Jesus answered, "Blessed are you, Simon Barjona! For flesh and blood has not revealed this to you, but my Father who is in heaven."

Truly, the deep things of the Spirit are not revealed to us on a mundane, flesh-and-blood level, for as Paul wrote to the church at Corinth, "The unspiritual man does not receive the gifts of the Spirit of God, for they are folly to him, and he is unable to understand them because they are spiritually discerned." And so they must be to us.

Jesus continued: " 'And I tell you, you are Peter, and on this rock I will build my church, and the powers of death shall not prevail against it. I will give you the keys of the kingdom of heaven, and whatever you bind on earth shall be bound in heaven, and whatever you loose on earth shall be loosed in heaven.' Then he strictly charged the disciples to tell no one that he was the Christ."

It was at the first meeting of Jesus and Simon that Jesus gave him the name Peter: " 'So you are Simon the son of John? You shall be called Cephas' (which means Peter)."

It was Peter's perception of the nature of Christ in Jesus—and Jesus' response to Peter's insight—that gave him the keys to the kingdom. That same perception gives us the keys today, enabling us to see that every man is innately the son of God, that the Christ in us is the eternal nature, "the only begotten son"; that we "are the temple of the living God; as God said, 'I will live in them and move among them, and I will be their God, and they shall be my people.' "

The True Church

"The groves were God's first temples," wrote William Cullen Bryant; and whoever walks or drives down a tree-lined lane, where the branches of the trees meet in graceful arcs above him, can well imagine the origin of the Gothic arches of traditional Christian churches. But the meeting place is secondary to the reason and the need for meeting. "The true church of Christ," says Charles Fillmore, "is a state of consciousness in man," although few have gone so far "as to know that in the very body of each man and woman is a temple in which the Christ holds religious services at all times."

Possibly the first step in this realization comes when we no longer think of the structure of bricks, stone, and mortar as being the true church. We seem to require outward things to represent mental concepts. But there dawns in our thought the awareness that the building would be meaningless unless there were people to worship in it; that all the appurtenances of faith are efforts to objectify thoughts of the mind, feelings of the heart, aspirations of the spirit in man.

Innately, perhaps subconsciously, many worshipful men would find points of agreement with Thoreau's assertion, "Every man is the builder of a temple called his body," and Carlyle's, "There is but one temple in the world, and that is the body of man" (quoted by author-architect Claude Bragdon in "The Beautiful Necessity"). And surely it is not merely by coincidence that obelisks, pillars, campaniles, and totem poles take the rudimentary form of man; that "at certain periods of the world's history, periods of mystical enlightenment," writes Bragdon, "men have been wont to use the human figure, the soul's temple, as a sort of archetype for sacred edifices." The most outstanding and architecturally beautiful cathedrals are designed thus; the nave corresponding to the human torso, the transept to the extended arms, and the altar, the very center of worship, corresponding to the location of the human heart.

With the passing of centuries, meaning often becomes overlaid with tradition and legend. No doubt this is true concerning the birth of Jesus. The very human story, mysterious enough in the facts of nature, is combined with that of the Christ nature.

We are told that Jesus was born differently from other infants; that His was a virgin birth. What that may mean has often been hidden from the very wise, and revealed to those of childlike faith and heart. Many minds have sought to unfold its meaning to our understanding. They tell us that "virgin" means simply "pure, innocent,"; that immaculate means "without stain or sin." And the poet Ella Wheeler Wilcox has ventured to declare that

"Whosoever is born of pure love
And comes desired and welcomed into the world,
Is of immaculate conception."

But is it not easy to understand, and so plain it seems amazing that we could miss it, that it is the Christ nature that is born virgin in every human soul? Jesus alluded to this mystical birth in the episode of Nicodemus' visit to Him by night. "Unless one is born anew, he cannot see the kingdom of God," Jesus tells him.

"How can a man be born when he is old? Can he enter a second time into his mother's womb and be born?"

Twice Born

Jesus tells Nicodemus that he must be born of water and of the Spirit.

It is by the birth of water that all mankind comes naturally into the world. It was from water that the first forms of life emerged in the steamy seas of a prehistoric earth; and the drama is repeated in our prenatal life. The second birth, the birth "of the Spirit," is the virgin birth, an inner quickening to spiritual perception that has no human father or mother, but only the consciousness of God as its source.

To think that Jesus had to be born differently from other children to become the illumined soul that from any viewpoint He truly was, would be discouraging; but faith permits us to believe that any soul that has gone as far in spiritual attainment as Jesus might be somewhat differently born.

We can think about, but we cannot really know of our own selves, all that is meant by the virgin birth until the Christ nature shall contrive to be born within us ourselves.

Surely, through all creation it has not been only for Mary, the mother of Jesus, that the heavens have rung with the glad song of the angels, nor for her alone to dream that a child growing beneath her heart might become a mighty counselor, savior, prince of peace. And however we view and think of the star of Bethlehem, wise men have always followed a star, a star of dedication and aspiration that should lead them eventually to the One; which is no less science than art.

The legendary manner of Jesus' birth, and of His death and resurrection, are matters whose meaning to different persons may be as varied as the differing attitudes of mind that characterize us all. The immediate, pragmatic, and practical challenge is not in untangling the impossible mixture of fact and legend of the historical Jesus, but rather the challenge of putting into practice the wisdom of His inspired teaching. To combine in our individual being what is meant by the nature of Jesus and the nature of the Christ is our great unfinished work. For as Charles Fillmore has said: "He was more than Jesus of Nazareth, more than any other man who ever lived on the earth. He was more than man, as we understand the appelation in everyday use, because there came into His manhood a factor to which most men are strangers. This factor was the Christ consciousness. The unfoldment of this consciousness by Jesus made Him God incarnate, because Christ is the mind of God individualized. We cannot separate Jesus Christ from God or tell where the man leaves off and God begins in Him. To say that we are men as Jesus was a man is not exactly true, because He had dropped that personal consciousness by which we separate ourselves from our true God self. . . . He became consciously one with the absolute principle of Being. He proved in His resurrection and ascension that He had no consciousness separate from that of Being, therefore He was this Being to all intents and purposes. Yet He attained no more than is expected of every one of us. 'That they may be one, even as we are one,' was His prayer."

Demonstrating the Law

"The explanation of all your problems, the explanation of your difficulties and the explanation of your triumphs in life boil down to this: *Life is a state of consciousness.* That is the beginning and the end. That is the final step in metaphysics. All the other steps but lead up to that," declares Emmet Fox.

What do we mean by consciousness? One meaning of the word is to be awake instead of being asleep (unconsciousness). We use the term to mean awareness. Imelda Shanklin defines consciousness as "a direct knowledge or perception of an object, state, or sensation." It is composed of all your ideas, all your beliefs, all the things that you accept as valid, founded on fact; the basis for what you believe or act upon in your personal life.

If you look at an object and think of it as you look at it, you are aware of it. You take a deep breath because the air is exhilarating, and you are conscious of the weather. You listen with rapt attention to music on the radio because the theme awakens a memory: you are conscious of the music. Or you may pass by an object, walk through the out-of-doors, hear but not hearken to the music, because your consciousness is focused elsewhere. In consciousness you are where your thoughts and feelings are. Thus in effect you are often closest of all to those whom you love the most and who love you in return, not necessarily because they are physically close by, but because they dominate your thoughts and feelings above other factors in your experience.

In the community where you dwell there are manifold ways of occupying your leisure time. You do not even know of some of them; you are oblivious or averse to others. Certain ones you seek out and respond to. Perhaps no two of us live in quite the same world, because we do not have identical consciousnesses. Out of the infinite possibilities of the manifest creation, you occupy a certain place, a place made up less of time and space than of consciousness. Change your consciousness, and you change your world—that is, the world to which you respond.

Your consciousness comprises your thoughts, feelings, attitudes; the way you look at things. Until you change this outlook on life, nothing else changes for you.

"What'er thou lovest, man,
That too become thou must:
God, if thou lovest God,
Dust, if thou lovest dust."

It is a basic Truth of life that things come to us, not by chance but by the law of cause and effect; as the manifestation of our consciousness. All that we are and have and do may be explained in terms of consciousness. There are other ways of accounting for the variances in the human condition, but they are anterior to this. The body in which we function, the house in which we live, the kind of work we do, the kind of people we meet, are the expression of our consciousness at the time.

To place in a world of sin, sickness, lack, and death a humanity endowed with the capacity to enjoy and the longing to attain to health, joy, bounty, and life, but with these forever out of reach—this could only be the work of some diabolical fiend! Yet this is what many people believe to be the work of God.

A Misconception

This conception of life is responsible for untold misery and sorrow. It has bathed the world in tears and has made the song of life a dirge to millions of men. Yet it is untrue. It is the tragic mistake that has been made in human minds. The world is not a world of sorrow unless we so conceive it and live it. There is not a good desire of the human heart but has its logical, legitimate, and possible fulfillment.

Desire is prophetic of its own fulfillment. The persistent desire and urge within man to overcome these negations is the soul's affirmation, "I can!" to the world's assertion, "You cannot!" Human problems, sickness, crises, death are not the execution of God's judgment but the effects of God-exclusion.

In a sinsick world of illusions, the persistent upward urge of the soul cries out against the falsity of what we fear and dread and suffer from. It is the evidence to material sense of a reality that transcends material sense. It is the voice of the higher self declaring the falsity of our belief in evil, and pronouncing God's work—as He did in the beginning—good. Heed that voice, live by it, persist in it, and gradually you will find the burdens lightened, the sorrows dispelled, as you claim your good and press your claim.

It is not possible to demonstrate change in body and affairs without undergoing a change within ourself. You always will and always must get the conditions that belong to your consciousness. You cannot cheat the laws of being. Men seldom deliberately choose sickness, misery, despair in life; but unwittingly they have chosen ways of thought, feeling, and attitude that invite these elements into their experience. Life is like an echo or a mirror that reflects back to us in form what we have radiated from within ourself.

Nothing can overcome you but your belief in your own weakness and futility. Nothing can make you strong but the discovery of your own strength. Claim your good and press your claim. Affirm, *"I am strong in the Lord, and in the power of His might."*

The thoughts of your mind, consciously or unconsciously entertained, are responsible for what appears in your experience as facts. The desires of the heart are the promptings of Spirit, ever urging you to think more truly. The two, mind and heart, must be united in purpose and activity, before the shadows can be dispelled and the light of God's good world be made to shine through the mist of appearances.

What is meant by "think more truly"? All that is real (true) in any experience is the good. The evil in things exists, but only in a relative or transient sense; that is, it exists to our consciousness or understanding, our point of view. In the absolute or enduring sense it has no reality. Its existence is comparable to the good as shadows to sunlight. "When the perfect [the good, the true] comes [in consciousness], the imperfect will pass away." Therefore to become free from the "shadow" of evil we must become increasingly conscious of the "light" of good. This is what Jesus meant when He said: "If your eye is sound, your whole body will be full of light; but if your eye is not sound, your whole body will be full of darkness. If then the light in you is darkness, how great is the darkness!"

Everything seems real to the state of consciousness to which it is related, but may be only a shadow of the reality of a higher plane of consciousness; as the shadow of a hand might be real to a shadow world but is only a poor intimation of what a hand is to the three-dimensional world.

Bring in the Light

To demonstrate the good we must be so much imbued with it that our sight is centered upon it, and evil ceases to exist except in the sense that we recognize it for what it is, a temporal appearance, a shadow, a picture upon a screen. To love goodness is not the same as to fear or combat evil. One does not fight shadows; one brings in light and the shadows are dispelled. Nor does it seem altogether practical to deny the appearance of evil, which often arouses the resistance of the intellect and merely gives us something else to work out. Better to acknowledge it for what it is, the projection of human thought: "Yes, I see it, but I do not accept it." As in a dream state, assailed by a terrifying adversary, I suddenly realize that I am only dreaming, and declare, "You have no reality. You only seem real because I have dreamed you into being. I will open my eyes and you will be gone!"

One of the commandments that Moses received from God (Exod. 20:16) was, "You shall not bear false witness." False witness is testimony to or acknowledgment of that which is false—the appearance of evil. "As for me and my house, we will serve the Lord," declared Joshua; which is another way of expressing the same concept. Or as a well-known metaphysical teacher once said, when asked if she expected another world war, "If it comes, it will not be by any power of thought and feeling I give to it!"

Regardless of appearances, our constant privilege and duty is to bear witness to what is true, honest, just, pure, lovely, of good report. "If there is any excellence, if there is anything worthy of praise, think about these things," as Paul admonished the Philippians.

Such an attitude toward life—the acceptance of a concept of universal laws, and the endeavor to apply them in individual experience—marks the difference between the type of religious belief that centers around the aggrandizement of an individual or religious hierarchy and the more pragmatic attitude of centering upon the application of the spiritual truths the right use of which made such leaders renowned. Thus, in seeking to apply the teachings of Christianity, we center our attention less upon the teachings *about* Jesus Christ than upon the teachings *of* Jesus Christ. For "you shall know the truth, and the truth will make you free," and "If you know these things, blessed are you if you do them," or again, "I will put my law within them, and I will write it upon their hearts; and I will be their God, and they shall be my people," as God said to the prophet Jeremiah.

"Gird thyself with incessant affirmatives." In whatever situation you are experiencing, think what in the nature of God and your eternal being is the Truth about it. Usually when you are concerned about human relations there is likely to be "your way, their way, and the right way," so you can arrive at a statement of Truth (an affirmation) that embodies the principle involved, and you may say "*All things conform to the right thing, under grace and perfect law.*" In the face of a physical or bodily challenge, you may conclude, *"This is the way it appears, but if it is not God's will for me it can be changed, and God's will for me is not infirmity but glowing life and health."*

None of us can make a thing true by affirming it to be true, if in the ultimate nature of things it is not true; but if in the sight of God it *is* true, then affirming that truth helps to make it true in fact and in personal experience, as it is in the eternal nature of being.

Trial and Error

The fact that somewhere in the remote past mankind elected to take the path of human experience, of trial and error, rather than the way of constant attunement to the will of God through incessant prayer and meditation, may account for many of the difficulties in which from time to time we find ourselves. But this is a fact too often used as an excuse for our shortcomings, rather than simply an explanation of them.

God, whose other name is love, "does not rejoice at wrong, but rejoices in the right." And as Paul said, "The written code kills, but the Spirit gives life." So it is not how many church services we attend, or how many study courses we have completed, but what we have learned actually to apply in daily living that brings us into a higher state of awareness. We must build a consciousness of the all-pervading good, and not be overcome by the appearance of evil.

Transiently (that is, in terms of consciousness) we are sons of earth; but eternally, in the true nature of being, we are sons of God and heaven. Most of our human striving is actually, though not always consciously, devoted to becoming consciously that which we eternally are; that which we see objectified in the person of Jesus, the Christ. And it is helpful to remind ourself repeatedly that Jesus is the name of the man of Nazareth, Christ a title to indicate the God-idea of perfect man; man in complete dominion as the "only [or truly] begotten son of the Father."

How shall we become like Him? How shall we transform consciousness so that it understands and expresses the divine idea?

If, day by day, we drop into the subconscious phase of mind the materials that will give us strength, then automatically, in the moment of our need as it arises, we shall find strength to meet the need. If we drop into the subconscious the materials that will give us patience, by the same token when patience is needed, we will find that we have it without even consciously recognizing it, so that if someone should remark that we seem to have more patience than most persons, it will surprise us.

What is meant by "dropping into the subconscious phase of mind" the materials or qualities we aspire to manifest?

Act on Convictions

It is very simple, though to say that it is simple is not quite the same thing as to say it is easy. Simply this: Act out in a small way what you would like to manifest in a large way. If you aspire to be calm and serene in large matters, cultivate the habit of meeting small matters calmly and serenely. If you tend to lose your temper easily, cultivate the habit of viewing the little vexing annoyances of every day with equanimity, even with a sense of humor. If you have a fear of the dark, cultivate the habit of thinking of all the lovely and pleasant things about darkness;

how seeds sprout in the darkness of earth; how falling asleep in the security and comfort of your darkened bedroom relaxes body, mind, and emotions from the activities of the day that is past, and prepares you for the day to come.

Whatever, in such ways, you drop into your subconscious phase of mind will "automatically, in the moment of your need as it arises," well up from the subconscious to strengthen and support you. The success of this way of demonstration is in action, not words. Act out in small ways what you want to attain to in large ways. Can you keep your poise when someone accuses you falsely of some shortcomings? When someone is late to an appointment? When there is a delay in traffic, or something goes wrong with your car? "I never become angry with people, but I certainly become annoyed with *things*!" is the testimony of one student who started working with this way of demonstration. Perhaps the opposite is true of other students. Both are on the way of attainment. Meeting small challenges in a poised, adult manner, giving things a light touch, prepares us for the larger issues of life.

Will power seems often to be disparaged among Truth students, yet rightly exercised it becomes the servant of man's demonstrable higher nature. Let a man have the will to find work if he is out of a job, and he is very likely to come up with not only a job but a superior position. Let him have the will to be well, and the innate forces of health within him respond to his clarion call. For the will to attain can become a constructive habit of man's inner nature, giving power and direction to his life.

By the same token, what might be called "won't power" can be a helpful complement to will power.

It is will power in disguise. When a man declares to himself, "I won't lose my temper," he is willing to control his temper. When he says, "I won't let my fear of strangers overcome me," he is saying in effect, "I reach out toward friendliness," or as some metaphysicians put it, "The Christ in me greets the Christ in you." But it must be a thought that does not stop with words. The Chinese have a saying that a picture is worth a thousand words. We might paraphrase this to assert that one action is better than a thousand words—unless the thousand words lead to an inspired right action. And another fortifying thought is contained in a saying you may have learned in Sunday School:

"Sow a thought, you reap a word.
Sow a word, you reap an act.
Sow an act, you reap a habit.
Sow a habit, you reap a character!"

Cause and Effect

"Are grapes gathered from thorns, or figs from thistles?"–Matt. 7:16.

"Do not be deceived; God is not mocked, for whatever a man sows, that he will also reap"–Gal. 6:7.

"The measure you give will be the measure you get"–Matt. 7:2.

"All who take the sword will perish by the sword"–Matt. 26:52.

"First the blade, then the ear, then the full grain in the ear"–Mark 4:28.

"What have I done that this should come upon me?" is an almost universal cry of beleaguered man. Usually it is a protest against a sense of injustice, as David cried out against Saul's enmity toward him ("What have I done? What is my guilt?") but it may be an unconscious and certainly unwilling recognition that somehow, regardless of appearances, things do not happen by chance, but by immutable law; that there is a cause for what happens *around us*, and that are most of all likely to be the cause of what happens *to* us. As one writer observes, things do not so much happen to us, as we happen to things.

Truly, it is the law that what we send out into the world tends to come back, increased and multiplied. In the next several paragraphs note of this action will be taken. For it is the law–yet indeed not all of the law.

The first law of life, so important that it is repeated six times in the first chapter of Genesis is, that everything brings forth–increases–"after its kind."

Every schoolboy knows this. If he has ever had a little garden he knows that radish seeds produce radishes, that you do not indeed gather grapes from thorns or figs from thistles; that what you sow, that also you will reap. The yield may vary from scanty to abundant dependent upon many variables such as sunshine, wind, and rain, the fertility of the soil; but the nature of the yield is predictable, it will follow the pattern of what has been sown. So sure can we be of this that if in the crop there appears something different from what we planted, we are still so certain of the law that we know that somehow the law of sowing and reaping, of cause and effect, has not been violated. Somehow the seed of what appears had been sown, either mixed by error among those we intentionally planted, or sown by the wind or in the droppings of a bird.

That this law applies no less to the inner man than to the outward world is attested by life no less than by Scripture. "To the pure all things are pure," declared Titus, and Solomon admonishes, "Keep your heart with all vigilance; for from it flow the springs of life." Jesus equated the thought of a thing with the performance of it when He declared, "You have heard that it was said, 'You shall not commit adultery.' But I say to you that every one who looks at a woman lustfully has already committed adultery with her in his heart."

This suggests to us that action is efferent as well as afferent; that causes originate in thought and feeling, as truly as thought and feeling can be the result of environment and circumstance.

In effect, then, every man creates his own world, his own heaven or hell, and dwells an angel or a devil therein. His is not precisely the same world as that of others—even of those who seem to be similarly involved, because no two of us are exactly alike, no two of us are in the same state of development, no two of us react in exactly the same manner to a shared experience.

"What is most important to you, then," as an Oriental philosopher has said, "is not so much the circumstances of your life as your attitude toward them."

"All reforms must begin with their cause," says Charles Fillmore.

Correct your thoughts and feelings and you correct your world.

Action and Reaction

It is a law of the physical world that for every action there is a correspondent reaction. "The world looks like a multiplication table, or a mathematical equation, which, turn it how you will, balances itself. Take what figure you will, its exact value, nor more, nor less, still returns to you," says Emerson. "Every secret is told, every crime is punished, every virtue rewarded, every wrong redressed, in silence and certainty. What we call retribution is the universal necessity by which the whole appears whenever a part appears. If you see smoke, there must be fire. If you see a hand or a limb, you know that the trunk to which it belongs is there behind."

"Which of you by being anxious can add one cubit to his span of life?" is a challenging question of the Master. If we think of "being anxious" in the usual sense, the answer must be, No one, or very few. But this is not to denigrate the power of thought, for man's deep-felt, earnest thought is indeed powerful, not only to change himself but to change the thoughts and consequent life patterns of others.

The pattern of cause and effect that has become established in our life tends to repeat itself until we "put on a new record." In the story of Elisha, the widow, and the cruse of oil, the pattern of lack needed to be changed to one of abundance (and even here, the law that things bring forth "after their kind" applies, for the increase took the form of the one thing the widow could claim to possess, a little oil).

"What shall I do for you?" was the prophet's question; a question which we must answer when we want to establish a new pattern of cause and effect.

Students often find that it helps them to define desires if they take a large piece of paper, draw a line down the center from top to bottom of the page. On the left side they list things they would like to have manifested (as effects) in their life. Recognizing outward manifestations as effects demands that they think of causes that will actualize these manifestations. On the right side of the line, then, they list mental equivalents of what they desire, possibly in the form of affirmations and denials. Added to these there should be a list of things they can do to bring about the desired results.

A variation of this procedure is called treasure-mapping. It consists of placing on a large sheet of paper—wrapping paper serves the purpose—pictures and words gleaned from magazines and newspapers that symbolize the heart's desire. As these are contemplated, often the user may be inspired with the thought of someone or something that can be a channel of fulfilment. Most frequently this involves some illumined thought, attitude, or action on his own part that contributes to the desired result.

Why do some persons attract more forms of blessing than others? May it not be in accordance to their observing, responding to, and appreciating? "For to him who has, (these developed qualities) will more be given; and from him who has not, even what he has will be taken away."

Look for Causes

The first place to look, in an endeavor to explain and understand certain unwanted conditions in our life, is for motivating causes in our thoughts, feelings, and attitudes. For most of them can rightly be explained on this basis. The fact that all such things cannot be completely explained does not justify us in rejecting all responsibility because it does not explain some—even some very important ones.

Some life experiences for which we are only secondarily responsible occur because of family relationships. When we are born into a family, as when we enter into a partnership or a marriage, we take on a responsibility which in the first instance may be unforeseen, but in the latter two should certainly be expected. "No man is an island." No man lives to himself alone. Even when he avoids human associations and becomes a recluse, a hermit, he is not exempt from the responsibilities arising from human relationships; he just rejects a relationship by which he might at least have a voice in decisions that involve him as a member of the human race. In many more specific, personal and closer areas of common need and fulfillment, is he not simply trying to reject what cannot be rejected—the unity of life?

Has he a sorrow? Who is there to share and thereby alleviate it? Has he a joy? Is there anything more hollow than the echo of a laugh?

Wittingly or unwittingly we are all "involved." Back of all more intimate involvements there is what has been called "race consciousness."

On the physical plane there is always action and reaction, cause and effect. (You stamp your foot, and in a least, infinitesimal degree the distant stars tremble!) In matters of human justice and injustice, war and peace, man's inhumanity to man, can we entirely deny participance? When issues affect our state, our nation, do we avoid responsibility by not carrying our share of the load? If someone else therefore must serve where we fail to do so, may we not still vicariously be required to meet some of the results that find their manifest expression in the one who accepts the task we rejected? "The scars are upon the soul," someone has said. And so, it might be added, are the records of all the good we do, every effort, even every aspiring thought and feeling. For what you strongly think and deeply feel tends always to carry over into manifestation. Jesus emphasized how important are the things we do or fail to do ("If you know these things, blessed are you if you do them"). The thoughts and feelings that motivate action may be of equal or even greater importance, because nothing can appear in the outward realm of circumstance that did not first appear in these inner realms.

In other words, no man can violate with impunity what his own aspiring nature demands of him.

Which brings us to another aspect of the law of cause and effect. It is called *karma*, a Sanskrit word signifying "the whole ethical consequence of one's acts, considered as fixing one's lot in the future existence." Its import is what might be called "the gospel of another chance." How many of us have said, "If only I could live my life over again I know I could do better, accomplish more, avoid some of the mistakes I have made this time!" Reincarnation is that opportunity. In fact it is an inescapable necessity, in fulfillment of the decree that "till heaven and earth pass away, not an iota, not a dot, will pass from the law until all is accomplished." Charles Fillmore puts it this way: "The teaching of Jesus is that all men shall, through Him, be made free from sin and be saved to the uttermost–spirit, soul, body. To give men opportunity to get the full benefit of salvation, life is necessary. So, when man loses his body by death, the law of expression works within him for reembodiment, and he takes advantage of the Adam method of generation to regain a body." "When man loses the material avenues of expression and has not developed the spiritual, he is in torment. Appetite longs for satisfaction." "Through repeated trials at living, man is finding out that he must learn to control the issues of life in his body."

The Inescapable Good

Perhaps it is unfortunate that in considering karma, its retributive aspects have been emphasized to the detriment of its blessings; for just as it is true that we cannot initiate negative causes in our life without undesirable reactions, so no good effort or accomplishment is unrewarded. Thus we find that certain souls come into this plane of life with talents so developed that they seem to do with little or no effort what may take others a lifetime to accomplish–and perhaps that is exactly what it has taken these specially gifted ones—a lifetime preceding the present one!

One of Charles Fillmore's comments is pertinent to this. He says: "Without doubt the secret of Paul's great illumination at the time of his conversion is that in previous lives he had built up a spiritual consciousness, and on his way to Damascus he 'stirred up' the gift that was within him. The new race that is now being born on this planet will develop these unused resources of the mind by realization, audible prayer, and thanksgiving and bring to the surface the riches of both the subconscious and the superconscious mind."

Anyone who is likely to read this volume is also very likely to have experienced intimations that what he is meeting now is the result of many past preparations, past experiences, acquired knowledge stored up in the subconscious (which survives the exigencies of rebirth). From it there occasionally well up fragments of what might be called "soul memory." There is a familiarity about places never before seen in the present life; a feeling of "always having known" someone we meet for the first time; knowledge of certain subjects to which we feel attracted but on which we are normally uninformed.

A Continuum

Life, it would seem, is a continuum. As we believe by faith or on the basis of what seems evidence and consequent conviction, that life will continue after somatic death, so the thought becomes almost inescapable that it did not begin at birth; that what we call a lifetime is only a segment of a larger life, as the present life is the succession of births and deaths. That is, we die to the body of infancy and are born to childhood, we die to childhood and are born to youth, and so on. All the physical elements of these successive bodies (which to human sense are one body) have as truly passed away as ever any shall, but they have been replaced so gradually, so much within the outward appearance of the body as we know it—so that for the most part we are unaware of these twin mysteries of death and birth by which we live.

All these aspects of the law of cause and effect: our own conscious and subconscious thoughts, feelings and attitude; our family, national, and racial relationships; our successive human embodiments—still do not account for some of the most exalting life patterns of man.

There is at least one more.

That one more is the life that assumes embodiment in this world not to balance his accounts on the ledger of debits and credits, lessons needed, lessons learned, but rather to serve, to give, to love; not under the law of necessity, but under the one law that supercedes it, the law of grace. This law is invoked when we utterly reject self-motivated thought and action, and throw ourselves upon the divine compassion of the Almighty, whose nature and action is love. Love is the great healer, the great redeemer. And back of all the causes that humanly we can identify, there is what has been called the First Cause—God. Giving, serving, growing, loving is the way of grace. Perhaps that is what Jesus really meant when he said that "love is the fulfilling of the law." "For this I was born, and for this I have come into the world, to bear witness to the truth."

Jesus Himself was, of course, the fulfillment of His own words, in His attainment of Christhood.

Through how many incarnations and how many times and lands had He come? And He has promised, even commanded, that the things He did we shall do also, and greater. Somewhere along the path, mankind substituted its own way for His way. "We are now living in a civilization dominated by human thought, and confusion is the result," says Charles Fillmore. "How many ages and aeons have passed since man lost (conscious) contact with God no one can tell. We have about six thousand years of recorded history and no heavenly conditions are recorded. Caves and sand drifts reveal the remains of man in combat with the gorilla for half a million years, with man himself sunk almost to the level of the monkey. . . . The great and most important issue before the people today is the development of man's spiritual mind and through it unity with God.

"God has given all things to us to use as we shall determine. We can use atomic energy to destroy or construct as we decree. . . . The one and only answer is that the moral and spiritual standard of the race must be raised the world over. . . . Every person must begin on himself and, as it dawns, let the light shine by imparting it to others. If this method were followed universally the millennium would be upon us in a marvelously short time."

In Returning

The answer is in returning again "home." Leaving the long and darksome path apart from Him, we shall find release from our troubles, lamps for our darkness, the oil of gladness for tears of sorrow. We shall find ourselves enwrapped in His everlasting arms of love; they shall uphold us and support us, and with His eye shall He guide us. With healing He shall heal us, and we shall be made whole. We shall wear sandals of understanding and the robe of righteousness; the crown of victory shall rest lightly on our brow. Our face shall be radiant as the sun, and our hearts shall be comforted.

We are children of God, full of grace and truth. The fearsome things we have believed of ourselves shall fade as mists before the sun of His manifest presence. We shall come before Him with singing. Our bodies shall be revealed in the image and likeness of Him who fashioned them from the beginning to be the temples of His indwelling, holy, perfect, without spot or blemish, without shadow of imperfection.

Our minds shall be, and indeed they are, one with His infinite mind. Our hearts shall be, and even now are, one with His great loving heart, giving and receiving love on every hand. We shall draw near to others and they to us in perfect accord because of Him. Our souls shall rise in triumph out of the dark night of illusion, fair as His own. All this and more shall be vouchsafed to us because even now we are turning toward Him, as He has ever turned toward us. We shall know and be known, and rest in knowing. The seal of His promise is upon us. The time of our deliverance is at hand. Old thoughts and old things shall be as waters that have passed away. We shall release old censures and condemnations of ourselves and others. No longer binding, we shall no longer be bound. We shall dwell as in a world defended from evil.

In ways as simple as this book, as wonderful as the birth of children, as beautiful as the evening star, as mysterious as our own life experiences, is the knowledge of God brought to man.

Meditation, Prayer, the Silence

"A prayer in its simplest definition is merely a wish turned Godward"–Phillips Brooks.

"Prayer is not overcoming God's reluctance; it is laying hold of His highest willingness"–Richard C. Trench.

"Good prayers never come creeping home. I am sure I shall receive either what I ask, or what I should ask"–Bishop Joseph Hall.

"The prayer of a righteous man has great power in its effects"–James 5:16.

"We kneel, how weak! we rise, how full of power!"–Trench.

Strong statements of Truth, in the form of affirmation and denial, become the lever by which man shall lift himself once more out of the pit that he has dug for himself. He shall know the Truth, and the Truth shall make him free.

"But if I am sick, how can I honestly deny this and say that I am well?" the student asks. You can say it first of all as an ideal of what you desire to call forth in your life. You can say it as a pattern by which to build.

Dr. H. Emilie Cady says: "Deny evil; affirm good. Deny weakness; affirm strength. Deny any undesirable condition, and affirm the good that you desire. This is what Jesus meant when He said, 'What you ask in prayer, believe [or claim and affirm] that you receive it, and you will.' This is what is meant by the promise: 'Every place that the sole of your foot will tread upon [or that you stand squarely or firmly upon] I have given to you.' "

As mistaken thoughts, feelings, words, and actions have filled man's life with woe, so true thoughts, feelings, words, and actions will bring about great improvements in life, through Jesus' example and teaching.

"All the nations of the world seek these things; and your Father knows that you need them," said Jesus. "Instead, seek his kingdom, and these things shall be yours as well."

Appearances do not always express the fullness of Truth. What we see as factual is inevitably influenced by location (as two persons viewing the same thing from different positions); vocation (a field of clover is something different to a farmer, a chemist, a botanist, an artist); mental and emotional consciousness (which may view an experience as everything from opportunity to disaster, rejoicing to despair).

A sick man in delirium may say of its mental pictures, "I know this is not true, but this is how it seems." So of many things that appear contrary to the promises and assurances of Christ, we may say something similar, and begin to correct the appearance by affirmation and denial. As Joel said, "Let the weak say, 'I am a warrior,' " and Paul, "Have this mind among yourselves, which you have in Christ Jesus."

Affirming what is basically false will not make it true. But affirming what is true will help us to express it. Likewise denying what is basically true will not change the truth, but denying what is thus false will help us to see the Truth.

Losing conscious contact with the creative forces

of being has brought the world close to disaster. "The great and most important issue before the people today is the development of man's spiritual mind and through it unity with God." Physical force, violence, riots, and warfare are outmoded as a way of settling differences and bringing about better conditions among individuals, races, and nations.

Common to All

There is a greater power which we must learn to invoke and rely upon as a guide to right action and fulfillment. It is the power of prayer and meditation. Prayer may be the only factor in our human experience that can save us and our world from self-destruction. Short of the fact that we are all human beings regardless of race or nationality, the one thing that is common to all is prayer. And people who consistently, sincerely, and unselfishly pray may well be the redemptive channels of man's deliverance from greed, arrogance, materialism, the lust for power, and the disregard for the rights of others.

"Prayer," writes Doctor Alexis Carrel, author of "Man the Unknown," "is a force as real as terrestrial gravity. As a physician, I have seen men, after all other therapy has failed, lifted out of disease and melancholy by the serene effort of prayer. It is the only power in the world that seems to overcome the so-called 'laws of nature': the occasions on which prayer has dramatically done this have been termed 'miracles.' But a constant, quieter miracle takes place hourly in the hearts of men and women who have discovered that prayer supplies them with a steady flow of sustaining power in their daily lives."

Prayer is a redemptive power as real as any known law of the so-called material universe.

How shall we define prayer? Emerson called it "the soliloquy of a beholding and jubilant soul, pronouncing God's work good." The familiar verse of James Montgomery puts it, "Prayer is the soul's sincere desire, uttered or unexpressed." Charles Fillmore describes it as "communion between God and man." Henry Ward Beecher declared "A man has a right to go to God by any way that is true to him. If you can think it out, that is your privilege. If you can feel it out, that is your privilege. One thing is certain; The child has a right to nestle in his father's bosom, whether he climb there upon his knee or by the chair by the side of him; any way, so that it is his father. Wherever you have seen God pass, mark it, and go and sit in that window again."

A popular painting called "The Omnipresence" portrays three robed figures in attitudes of prayer. One is kneeling, head bowed, hands clasped. Another stands erect, but with head still bent and hands still clasped. The third figure stands erect, head thrown back, eyes looking upward, with arms outstretched.

There are times in the twilight of the soul when only a kneeling posture seems to express the soul's anguished sense of need and importunity. And it is perhaps the soul's need more than God's demand. There are yet other times when the sense of burden is indeed lifted, and yet the soul stands in reverent awe before the mystery and wonder of the Creator and His creation. And there is yet a third attitude of the soul, that in the language of the body reaches outward and upward in joyous realization and thanksgiving.

A Higher Power

Whatever in us invokes the help of a power higher than our own conscious abilities to meet problems, situations, opportunities, may be described as prayer. And the description seems to apply not only to the religious-minded, but to those who call themselves atheists and agnostics. These too generally recognize that a machine did not create itself, nor man himself; that there is something higher than man—at least higher than man generally credits himself with being—and when he has exhausted his acknowledged human resources, he appeals to "whatever gods there be," to chance, to luck, to the unknown, to the innate, to the creative forces, to the higher mind, the Christ Mind, to the superconscious, or the subconscious, or infinite intelligence, or the Absolute.

The name he gives to Whatever-it-is man appeals to doesn't seem to make much difference in the results he gets; results apparently depend more upon his faith and convictions, or even upon his nonresistance, than upon theology or logic.

It is the common experience of all of us who pray that the more we pray the less urgent our prayers become, and with less need for urgency. From asking or demanding something from a higher Power, there evolves a feeling of confidence in the nature of that Power, so that there is the desire to bask in Its presence as one basks in the sun's warmth and light. From trying to change things from the way they appear to us, we seek to envision how things appear in the sight of God. And so we come through prayers of demand and petition to prayers of meditation or communion where human questioning is silenced, into the affirmation of what we conceive to be God's Truth and goodness.

In the Scripture, we take patterns of prayer from the prophets of the Old Testament, and predominantly from Jesus in the New Testament.

Jesus called the higher Power that He appealed to God. And to Him God was Father. To Jesus the presence of God was so real, so close, so immediate, as to be a Presence more vivid than that of the human personalities who so often surrounded Him. A spiritual awareness that we attain to only in moments of special effort and concentrated attention was habitual with Him. The gospel writers do not analyze Jesus' method. They only report results. Someone is in trouble and Jesus responds to the need. He is seen to have had "compassion for them." He says, "Be clean," to the leper, and the leper is cleansed; to the lame, "Take up your pallet and walk," and it is so; to the blind, "Go, wash in the pool of Siloam," and sight is restored.

A Pattern of Prayer

In the account of His raising of Lazarus we are made more aware of successive steps in prayer than anywhere else in the Gospels (except in what is commonly called "The Lord's Prayer").

It will be recalled that Lazarus had been dead for four days when Jesus arrived at his tomb, accompanied by Lazarus' sisters, Mary and Martha, who chided Him at His tardiness in reaching them. News of the wonders performed by Him had reached the village of Bethany, and a crowd awaited His arrival.

In retrospect we picture the scene: the wailing women, the curious crowd, the grim, gray, rock-hewn cave, with a circular stone rolled across the opening. We are touched again by Jesus' compassion. He weeps, but He does not stop at weeping. We hear Him again addressing God, as if He were an immediate, close, available, mighty, and loving Presence: "Father, I thank thee that thou hast heard me. I knew that thou hearest me always, but I have said this on account of the people standing by, that they may believe that thou didst send me." So deep and strong is His sense of the Father's presence that He is apologizing for voicing His appeal aloud.

For us this account of the greatest healing miracle in Holy Writ serves a purpose that the Gospel writers may not have anticipated.

It gives us a basic pattern for prayer, in six explicit steps.

1. *"Take away the stone."* In every prayer that seeks betterment for ourselves or others, the very first step is to remove whatever barrier exists in mind and heart, to open our minds to betterment; to agree that improvement is possible, to consent to whatever changes this may demand of ourselves (for prayer does not change God, but rather the one who prays), to accept the good in the form that God offers it.

2. *"Jesus lifted up His eyes."* He lifted His vision as well as His sight. If He had seen Lazarus as the others saw him, that is, in the same acceptance of death and corruption, He could not have called forth Lazarus to life. Lazarus' sister Martha testified, "Lord, by this time there will be an odor, for he has been dead four days." The "four days" made the death official in the judgment of the Jewish authorities, and it may be that Jesus delayed in responding to the appeal to raise His friend to life again so that it might be accepted as a true miracle (the miracle which to human sense sealed Jesus' doom, and

ushered in "the week that changed the world").

In the highest form of prayer we do not ask that God lower His sight to ours, but rather we seek to raise our sight to His.

3. *"Father, I thank thee."* In the Bible Jesus knew, which we call the Old Testament, giving thanks to God was almost as much a part of daily life as breath itself. Jesus was reared in this thought. He knew much of the Scriptures from memory. But whereas it might have become almost automatic therefore to begin a prayer with giving thanks, somehow as we picture the scene–the cold gray tomb from which the confining stone is being rolled away, the mourning crowd more curious and doubting than faith-filled–the words come alive! And it is when such words come alive in us that they are effectual to us. They become the testimony of remembered blessings, our faith in those to come.

4. *"He cried with a loud voice."* Reason could not expect nor indeed explain this miracle of faith fulfilled, as reason cannot adequately explain the miracles of answered prayer in the present-day world which tends to make science its god. Why a *loud* voice? It was a voice of unquestioning assurance. But also the term *loud* is a commentary on the narrator. It may be that indeed it was actually in a loud voice that Jesus spoke; but had He uttered the words, "Lazarus, come out!" in a whisper, the words would be as thunder in the understanding of the hearers, if not to their ears!

5. *"The dead man came out."* The things that are impossible to mortal man are possible to God, and become possible to God-filled man, whose devoted cry echoes through many voices down the years: "One thing I know, whereas I was blind, now I see:

whereas as I was dead I am come alive again, whereas I was impoverished I am enriched, whereas I was abandoned and rejected, I am loved and accepted. Old thoughts and old things are become as waters that are passed away: behold, all things are made new."

6. *"Unbind him, and let him go."* Even though we may have come out of death, or the very valley of the shadow of it, the action of faith is not complete until we depart from the ways of thought, feelings, and attitudes that brought about our sorry plight. Though the actual burden is gone, though the problem, whatever it was, has let go of us, it is of equal importance that we let go of it. Too many of us dwell in and relive the hard winter of financial depression, the sorrow of a bereavement that was actually a release and freedom for the one about whom we grieve, the tensions and stresses of a surgical experience which boasts of its exceptional factors. Loose them and let them go! And if we are holding another in the remembrance of the possibly challenging steps by which he has come to the present time, let us echo Jesus' words with meaning, "I free him and let him go!"

The Human Jesus

It is notable that Jesus' biographers do not conceal the fact that Jesus, though He was the very Christ incarnate, had human emotions and expressed them on several other occasions besides the raising of Lazarus. Matthew quotes His parable: "We piped to you, and you did not dance; we wailed, and you did not mourn." We are given glimpses of His dark hours: Luke describes His prayer in the Garden of Gethsemane, when He asked God that "this cup" be removed from Him, and "being in an agony, he prayed more earnestly; and his sweat became like great drops of blood falling down upon the ground." The writer to the Hebrews tells us that He "offered up prayers and supplications, with loud cries and tears" and "he learned obedience through what he suffered."

These are, however, exceptions to the rule, exceptions that serve to remind us that He was not only divine but divinely human as well. Even in the dark hours, His sorrow was more for others than for Himself. In His darkest hours on the cross, and in His other prayers of petition, they were never begging in character, but imbued with an impressive sense of His talking heart to heart, eye to eye with the Creator. Charles Fillmore comments that the Lord's Prayer, which we so universally use, in the original is a series of affirmations.

The Lord's Prayer

It is spoken by millions of people daily, and often it is spoken by rote. It would be a mighty agency for spiritual quickening if faithfully thought about and devotedly applied. Jesus must have attached great importance to it when He offered it as a model prayer, saying, "Pray then like this."

Speak this Prayer with deep feeling daily for a month, and you will discover definite improvement in your life and your attitude toward life. Good will flow through your life as health, as guidance, as supply.

Let us follow through the words of this immortal prayer and consider what they mean to us.

"Our Father."

As contrasted with the view of deity held by many

earlier teachers, Jesus thought of God quite simply as Father. Significantly, too, He did not say simply "my Father" or "your Father," but "our Father," thereby linking us all with Him in common brotherhood. How much is implied in that! He has told us of the power of the Father; that not He, Jesus, but God the Father did the mighty works of healing, and prosperity, and right adjustment manifested through Him. Does He not say to us in effect: "My brethren, what I do you shall do and can do, for God is not only My Father but your Father also. Have faith in His power within you as I have faith in His power through Me, and all things shall become possible unto you"?

"Who art in heaven."

Does God seem a long way from you? Do you still address Him as if He were remote and a stranger? Remember the teaching of Jesus: "The kingdom of God is in the midst of you" and "The kingdom of heaven is at hand."

"The God I know is a God close by,
Not seated on throne in far-off sky . . .
In children's prattle, in manhood's prime,
Since the birth of words until end of time.
For the God I know with a thought that's free
Is the God of love, found in you and me."

"Hallowed be thy name."

What is God's name? When He commissioned Moses to call His children out of bondage in Egypt, He said, "Say this to the people of Israel, 'I AM has sent me to you.' " How do we hallow that name? By linking it with only that which we conceive to be of God. Thus let us not say, "I am sick, I am weak, I am poor"; for I AM is never sick, weak, or poor. And what is God's name for His manifestation? His name for all things, as He created them in the beginning, is "good." He beheld all that He had made and pronounced it "very good." Shall our own name for things be less? Shall we condemn and pass judgment of evil when God Himself did not? "The people imagine a vain thing," and the vain imagining of people fills the world with ills. Let us not link the name of God for Himself or for His manifestation with lack or distress, which are unlike Him. Let us hallow His name, the I AM, in ourself by keeping it holy and wholly unto Him.

"Thy kingdom come."

God's kingdom is at hand and within us, we are told. It is within ourself that we must call that kingdom into expression. We do this when we make the standard of the kingdom the standard of our thought and feeling. Let us think with kingdom-of-heaven charity and tolerance, let us act with kingdom-of-heaven kindness, let us give kingdom-of-heaven service in our business dealings, let us speak the kingdom-of-heaven Truth in love, wisdom, and good judgment.

You are the ruler of your own world of body, soul, and spirit; your thoughts and emotions are the children of your kingdom. Speak with kingly authority and live up to your kingly estate, remembering that though you are king in your own kingdom, you are also subject to and son of another King.

"Thy will be done."

Many persons cannot say this, really thinking it as they say it, without flinching. It is as if in speaking these words they were inviting calamity. Is the will of God for man so terrifying? Hardly. No sadder mistake in religious conceptions has ever been made than that which views all disasters and calamities as the will of God, sent by Him to punish and afflict His erring children. As a matter of fact the opposite is true. Man brings evil upon himself by his own misunderstanding and misdeeds. God continually wipes out the ills with His blessing, even to the sending of His only-begotten Son to heal the sick, raise the dead, and cast out the demons of false belief and terror from the minds and lives of men.

God's will is not something to fear but something to trust. We who imagine that we know our own good so well have only to add a little constructive phrase to our own decree in order to embrace the will of God and cleanse our thought of fear.

When you can specify of any good that you desire, "This, O loving Father, is my good as I see it—give me this or what in Your sight is better," you are invoking the will of God. His will for us is always the highest good. Seldom is our own vision as yet so clear as to reveal all the splendor of His perfect will. We see it only as through a glass, darkly. Hence let us ask always that we may be receptive not alone to our good as we see it but to our good as God sees it.

"As in heaven, so on earth."

As within, so without. All growth is of this kind. "First the blade, then the ear, then the full grain in the ear." The kingdom of God is within us, but as we give it recognition we must also give it manifestation so that it may be on earth—on the outer plane—as it is in heaven, on the inner plane of thought and feeling.

Heaven and earth are not separate. They are one, as the two sides of a leaf are one, as seed and fruit are one. Heaven is the seed of the earth. Earth must be the fruit of heaven. As a man thinks within himself, so he becomes in manifestation. As we think and feel—or become more clearly conscious of—heaven, we shall manifest more and more of our heavenly nature. This is our great purpose in life. We must be about it, for it is the Father's business in us.

"Give us this day our daily bread."

There is bread, and bread: bread of earth and bread of heaven. Perhaps to most of us who repeat the Lord's Prayer this passage is not a petition for food for the physical body, for most of us have more than enough of material food. Generally we are better fed physically than we are spiritually, not because the spiritual supply is lacking—although some of us may not know where to find it—but because we are not always conscious of spiritual needs or aware that this passage in the Lord's Prayer has an application to such needs. Bread is a symbol of nourishment. It has been called the staff of life. A. S. M. Hutchinson in his book "The Soft Spot" suggests that this passage may be applied to whatever need we discern in our life. Our body may be well fed. Our mind may be stuffed with facts and information, but we may need spiritual sustenance very much. "Give us this day our daily bread" becomes then a prayer for spiritual sustenance. It may be that we are well aware of the spiritual values of life yet have not learned how to build them into our moral fiber in such a way as to strengthen it.

Whatever our need may be, we can pray, "Give us this day our daily bread." If it is peace and tranquillity, we can still pray, "Give us this day our daily bread" as serenity of soul. If it is energy we need, or prosperity, or rest, again we can pray, "Give us this day our daily bread," for it is a prayer for nourishment of the needy, a prayer that states the need but leaves the answer with God.

Like the manna that fell from heaven (and unlike most material resources), the spiritual forces of our life require continual renewal. They are always present but they must be continually transmitted through us into expression. We cannot live today by yesterday's virtue or morality, but the strength built up through the yesterdays must be given continual renewal in today. Spiritual qualities cannot be taken for granted. They must be exercised.

The prayer for nourishment of daily needs, though it may become familiar to us, never grows old in the sense of being outworn. It is as vital today and every day as in any day of the past.

"And forgive us our debts, as we also have forgiven our debtors."

This passage of the prayer perhaps more than any other clearly indicates the way in which God's law operates. It states the condition upon which our relationship to His manifestations depends. The Master showed very clearly that the operation of God's law is not dependent upon man's caprice or upon anything but practical faith in action, a recognition of Truth, and compliance with the mode of its manifestation. Lloyd C. Douglas in his book "Forgive Us Our Trespasses" uses an illustration that makes this very clear. He describes a man as owing a debt that he is unable to pay. The debtor says in effect: "I would gladly pay you if I could. But my debt to you is greater than I can possibly pay. I know that you do not need what I owe, and yet I know that it is right that I should pay my debt." The creditor in turn says, "Very well, if you will cancel the debts that others owe to you I will cancel your debt to me."

What we owe to God, God does not need for Himself. He does not demand that we suffer for mistakes that we have made nor does He gain pleasure or profit from our suffering. It is His will that love and understanding and forgiveness shall wipe out the sins and sorrows of the world. So with all patience and wisdom He says to us, "If you will cancel the debts that others owe to you, your debt to Me is canceled." In other words, we must wipe out misunderstanding and wrongdoing and condemnation. We must not hold others under such bondage, for we not only cause them sorrow but we bind ourself by the same unforgiveness with which we bind them.

Surely the whole world is eventually to see the wisdom of compliance with this law. Do you not think it possible that the great Master who looked so deeply into the hearts and lives of men and whose vision extended so far beyond that of others in point of penetration, sensed beforehand the great needs and problems of the world that were to arise out of their greediness and hardness of heart, their lust for power and money? Surely, doing so, He could offer no more telling counsel than this: "Forgive us our debts, as we also have forgiven our debtors."

And what would you be forgiven? There are many kinds of debts besides money debts. There are debts of gratitude, of service, of kindliness, of remembrance, and a thousand others. Perhaps none of us can ever repay those who have in some way blessed us for all that they have done, but we can pass on the spirit of their service. Those who give in the Christ spirit do not expect necessarily to be compensated by those whom they have served, but if those who have received blessings will share their blessings, somehow in the great ongoing all will give and all will receive "good measure, pressed down, shaken together, running over."

"And lead us not into temptation."

Ferrar Fenton offers an alternative translation of this passage: "Abandon us not to trial." We should like to change the preposition *to* to *in*—"Abandon us not in trial"—as more truly expressive of present understanding of the nature of God, who we believe does not abandon us in time of trial but is mightily with us to guide and bless and strengthen us if we find ourself tempted of evil. Every time of temptation is truly a time of opportunity for us to find God's righteous answer to the problem presenting itself. Always we have within us by His grace a power that is greater than any seemingly adverse power in the world. A part of our great adventure in life is the discovery of how God's power may be applied to give us the dominion that He promised us in the beginning.

So when we pray the Lord's Prayer, we do not say, "lead us not into temptation," but, "Leave us not in temptation."

"But deliver us from evil."

To Occidental students this reading seems better than the personalizing of evil implied in "deliver us from the evil one." The sense of the entire passage is "You do not abandon us to trial but deliver us from evil."

On this strong note the prayer as Jesus gave it ends. The customary closing realization "For thine is the kingdom, and the power, and the glory, for ever and ever, Amen" is not given in the Bible text. It was added, says Charles Lewis Slattery in "How to Pray," by the Church, after our Lord's earthly ministry, as an ascription suitable for liturgical use.

All Prayer is Good

Our prayers become a transforming power in our life when we link their meaning with life's experiences. Any attempt at prayer is better than none at all. Any attitude or posture of prayer, any words of prayer, either those composed by others or words of our own, and even any partial attention that may be given to them, is better than no prayer at all. But that prayer is most effective in our life which we most easily and completely think and feel. When we deeply feel our prayers and link them with the circumstances of life, they become a vitalizing, quickening factor in our life. Prayers of realization are mightier than prayers of supplication. Supplication implies a lack of something which must be begged of God. Prayers of realization acknowledge that even before we ask He has answered, that we have already been given what we need, and that our part is to realize the Truth and accept it with thanksgiving.

Whether our prayers are prayers of rote or the spontaneous outpouring of the mind and heart, the essential thing is that they should be really thought and felt, and that they should be an earnest effort definitely to contact the source of our being, to align ourself with God's purpose and His love, to make not only our words but our thoughts, emotions, and actions the channel for His expression.

Even speaking true words that we do not really feel is helpful sometimes. Merely hearing them mentally may serve to startle us into recognition of their truth, or may gradually change the tenor of our beliefs and make them more constructive. That prayers do not change God must be patent to our understanding. That God does not so much listen to our words as look upon our heart, and that the transforming power of prayer is from within outward, must be the basis of whatever improvement we see in our circumstances through the power of prayer. A true understanding and application of this power will open the floodgates of prosperity and joy to us. There is no stint or limit in the mind of God. He withholds no good thing from us. His blessings are manifold and are free for all to enjoy, but we must make our compliance with the law of their expression as free and wholehearted as we wish results to be.

Our Lord's Prayer, when prayed with wholehearted attention and understanding, will be found to be amazingly complete, a model prayer indeed. We should use it more rather than less, but also we should use it more thoughtfully and devoutly.

In prayer Jesus was simply reaffirming what He already deeply knew to be the truth of being. Will prayer change God? Will it change natural law? No, certainly with God "there is no variation or shadow due to change." He shows no partiality. If human petition or decree could change God this would result in chaos. But while it will not change natural law it will invoke a hitherto unknown action of natural law in such a way as to seem miraculous, and reveal the application of a universal principle to a specific need. For now "our knowledge is imperfect and our prophecy is imperfect," but when His nature is fulfilled in us, we shall see with understanding, or as face to face with the Almighty.

Spiritual Healing

"It is not the will of my Father who is in heaven that one of these little ones should perish"–Matt. 18:14.

"Do not be conformed to this world but be transformed by the renewal of your mind, that you may prove what is the will of God, what is good and acceptable and perfect"–Rom. 12:2.

"Do you not know that you are God's temple and that God's Spirit dwells in you?"–I Cor. 3:16.

"The power of the Lord was with him to heal"–Luke 5:17.

"Who forgives all your iniquity, who heals all your diseases"–Psalms 103:3.

"Then shall your light break forth like the dawn, and your healing shall spring up speedily"–Isa. 58:8.

"Spiritual healing." Is there really any other kind? "God healed him. I bound up his wounds," is the testimony of a physician.

There is only one healing power in all the world, and that is a power to create new cells and eliminate old ones, a power that is possessed by the innate intelligence or creative forces in living organisms, however evoked.

It is the same power, whether it is invoked by a physician or a metaphysician, an affirmation or medication. The healing power is no respecter of persons. It is the same regardless of race or religion. It is the same for Jew or Gentile, pagan or Christian. It is the same in ancient and in modern man. Often its nature is misunderstood. The patient of the witch doctor may believe that it is the pagan ritual, the beating of the tom-toms, or the nauseous concoctions that he is required to imbibe that benefit him. The modern physician relates the healing power to his medications, the metaphysician to his prayers.

To a certain degree all are right. For it is probably in these agencies only secondarily, and sometimes not at all, but surely and certainly in the patient's *response* to these very diverse methods that healing is attained. And though faith is a great factor in human response, some of these methods are effective where no active faith in the afflicted person is discernible. They are effective, apparently, in the degree that they act as a stimulus to the innate restorative powers within the patient's organism.

Disease is not, strictly speaking, a thing in itself. It is the absence of something. Health is a natural state. Its apparent absence, or an interference with it, we call disease. But disease is like darkness. Darkness is not a thing in itself; it is the relative absence of light. Light is positive; it is a thing in itself. When you bring in light, what becomes of the darkness; where does it go? Nowhere. What becomes of it? It is nonexistent. Light, on the other hand, is real. We measure the space between the stars and galaxies in terms of "light-years," the distance over which light can travel in a year's time, which is approximately 6,000,000,000,000 miles. We do not measure things in terms of darkness.

The Innate

No method of healing can create new cells within the body of a living organism. Only the creative forces in the body can do this. The organism tends to maintain itself if it is not interfered with. The creative forces are self-sufficient. They need no help. They just need "no interference," or the removal of obstructions that impede their natural action. To clear the way for the innate, creative forces, then, is the true purpose of healing agencies.

Masaharu Taniguchi, in his book "You Can Heal Yourself," describes what he believes takes place in these words: "We are inclined to think of medicine as something distinct from mental therapy, but actually there is no therapy outside of mental therapy. Regardless of whether the disease is internal or external, therapy takes place through the creation of new cells by the inner intelligence. Matter does not have the intelligence and power to transform itself into cells. Thus mind is the only effective therapist. A small amount of observation will make this point clear to us. Physicians can do no more than provide the best possible condition for the operation of the therapeutic power dwelling in man." This, however, is not to denigrate the skill and training of the dedicated practitioner of medicine or of any other agency that can serve as a channel of recovery. But "the point which students of mental therapy often overlook is that all disease arises through the action of mind in the same way that its cures take place through mental activity."

The law of healing is a demonstrable principle, as effective today as it was two thousand years ago in the time of Jesus, or in the centuries that reach back to man's initial dawning consciousness; and it manifests for each individual according to his consciousness.

Life is an eternally acting, eternally manifesting principle. Life gives to every man opportunities to experience the regenerating and restorative powers innate within him. He uses the life principle according to his consciousness, inviting either health or sickness. Thoughts, feelings, attitudes, actions that are constructive or destructive in nature all invite parallel or corresponding states in the body. The individual who is "strong in the Lord" (or law) of his being will not succumb to the attacks of adverse microorganisms as will the person whose innate energies and resources are weakened by fear, hatred, jealousy, and other destructive factors in his experience.

Where the Trouble Lies

When a person seeks help from a human authority he is likely to say, "I am in trouble." It would be more nearly true if he were to say, "Trouble is in me." His will is to be well, and his willingness to accept the responsibility that he shares in recovery, are paramount factors in restored well-being. In this era of modern science most practitioners of whatever background and training recognize the psychosomatic factor. Even centuries ago Shakespeare voiced this principle when he had Petruchio saying, "'Tis the mind that makes the body rich."

One of the greatest discoveries of modern times—and the least heralded or acclaimed—is the mental law of cause and effect. So universal is its action seen to be, that where there is an apparent exception we are inclined to question it. When we see someone experiencing ill health or some other misfortune, we are inclined to take it for granted that he has, either consciously or unconsciously placed himself in an undesirable relationship to the laws of his own well-being. As Emerson put it, "Cause and effect, means and ends, seed and fruit, cannot be severed; for the effect already blooms in the cause, the end preexists in the means, the fruit in the seed."

We would like to think that we are exceptions to this law. We are tempted to try a shortcut, or an easier way out than acceptance of the obvious conclusion that in some manner we are not conforming to procedures that produce results we desire. We would like to shift the responsibility. Perhaps a physician can give us a pill or potion, a metaphysician can prescribe a mantram or affirmation that will do what is required. Anything but to change our ways! Yet changing our ways may not be as drastic or as difficult as we anticipate; and beyond the required self-discipline it may soon even be pleasant, and will be eventually, beyond doubt.

The conscious direction of the mind toward healing of the body would seem to be the most direct and natural healing agency, and one whose results become more and more powerful as regular times of meditation and prayer establish a conviction of the true nature of healing, and a confidence in the innate creative forces within us all. For improvement is not attained by wishful thinking, or by will power, but by one's convictions. When he is convinced that healing is possible, that he deserves to be well, and that all the forces of his own being as well as the will (plan) of God are "for him" to be well, he removes roadblocks in consciousness and clears the way.

Many physicians have taken note of the remedial power of meditation and prayer in evoking the latent forces of healing.

"True prayer," writes Dr. Alexis Carrel, "represents a mystic state when the consciousness is absorbed in God. This state is not of an intellectual nature. Also it remains inaccessible as incomprehensible to the philosophers and to the learned. Just as with the sense of beauty and of love, it demands no book knowledge. The simple are conscious of God as naturally as of the warmth of the sun, or the perfume of a flower." And of the healing power of prayer, "It is only in the cases where all therapeutics are inapplicable or have failed, that the results of prayer can be surely proved . . . Prayer has sometimes, so to speak, an explosive effect. Patients have been cured almost instantaneously of affections such as lupus of the face, cancer, kidney troubles, ulcers, tuberculous of the lungs, of the bones or peritoneum. The phenomenon is produced nearly always in the same way. Great pain, then the feeling of being cured. In a few seconds, at most a few hours, the symptoms disappear and the anatomic lesions mend. The miracle is characterized by extreme acceleration of the normal processes of healing."

The quiet miracles of prayer take many forms: releasing the pressure of mental and emotional tensions in some form of confessional, by confiding repressed thoughts and feelings to a doctor, friend, or counselor, or by "writing a letter to God"; silent communion with nature; physical exercise; some creative hobby such as woodcarving, clay modeling, handicrafts (Dr. John Rathbone Oliver, in his book "Fear," tells of the redemptive value of such occupations for businessmen, harassed by vocational pressures); and finally service to others considered less fortunate than ourselves.

In all of these forms of therapy the individual "loses himself" or "is transported" into another world, fulfilling the concept that to be all wrapped up in ourselves is loss, to lose ourselves in some constructive emprise that "takes us out of ourselves" is gain, which might be considered a rough paraphrase of Matthew 10:39: "He who finds his life will lose it, and he who loses his life for my sake will find it."

The Inner Splendor

There is a second element in common to these quiet miracles of prayer. They are all based on giving, on releasing, on letting go, on radiating something of the inner splendor that Browning acclaimed, in creative and constructive ways. And giving is a kind of invitation to life.

What happens when we pray? "Pray for one another, that you may be healed. The prayer of a righteous man has great power in its effects" James declared. Our conviction of the effectiveness of prayer is based empirically upon the observed alleviation of conditions for which prayers are made, but basically upon the premise that health and well-being is the natural expression of the creative forces in us all; that when we clear our thought and feeling we open the way for the natural order to appear; that since the nature of the power that heals is mental, the most direct appeal to that nature is mental; that the effects of prayer are in proportion to the conviction with which they are made: that though on the plane of the conscious phase of mind we appear to be all separate, on the superconscious level we are one, like the spokes of a wheel which on the rim are apart, but converge at the hub; and that it is apparently on the subconscious plane that the therapy of prayer is most effective.

When we pray for others, then, we are not seeking to bombard them with our personal will. Instead, we seek to "clear the way," yielding the energy of our loving thought and feeling as channels of blessing.

The inquiring mind of man, in cases of answered prayer as in countless other subjects that command his attention, is not content to know what happened. He wants to know how.

Let Your Light Shine

Such a man is a certain Unity minister. Twice a week for many years in stated services he has led a congregation in prayers for healing, guidance, prosperity. Frequently reports of healing were made. What, he often asked himself, really happened in such prayers? Finally the thought occurred to him: "Instead of asking myself about this, why don't I ask God, just as I ask Him for help in so many other ways?" Then, as he was leading the congregation in audible statements of prayer, he silently asked God, "Is this simply mental soothing syrup? Is anything beyond the consoling and relaxing thought of the moment actually accomplished?" (But let it be said that consoling and relaxing thought are in themselves therapeutic.)

As with deepening earnestness he continued praying, he says, "it was as if little lights appeared above the heads of the worshipers. I understood this was the outpicturing of spiritual energy or realization generated by the devotion of the persons praying. As the prayers continued, these lights seemed to swirl and rise and come together above our heads, like a rush of visible wind and disappear in a kind of cloud. I interpreted this as meaning that our part was simply to pray, and that the creative forces of Being would direct the energy thus generated to whomever and whatever persons and conditions needed it most."

Peace in a Troubled World

"Give us the faith to believe that when God wants us to do or not to do any particular thing, God finds a way of letting us know it"—Peter Marshall.

"When the Son of man comes, will he find faith on earth?"—Luke 18:8.

"Be glad of life because it gives you the chance to love and to work and to play and to look up at the stars; to be satisfied with your possessions but not content with yourself until you have made the best of them; to despise nothing in the world except falsehood and meanness, and to fear nothing except cowardice; to be governed by your admirations rather than your disgusts; to covet nothing that is your neighbor's except his kindness of heart and gentleness of manners; to think seldom of your enemies, often of your friends, and every day of Christ; to spend as much time as you can with body and spirit in God's out-of-doors—these are little guidepaths to peace"—Henry Van Dyke.

Millions of people have found deep peace of soul and body through meditation and prayer; by inviting spiritual guidance, and following it faithfully; by forgiving themselves and others their shortcomings; by employing such affirmative prayers as: *"I am now in the presence of pure Being, and immersed in the holy spirit of life, light, and love. I am positive against all that is beneath (unworthy of) me, receptive to all that is above."*

How is this possible in a world that is torn by dissention, aggression, warfare? Can man truly find peace in a troubled world? Are we not all caught up in the mass consciousness of humanity? Although we are all involved in and to some degree responsible for the world's woes, their effects upon us vary according to our individual consciousness. In times of challenge all that we have learned in the past, all the overcomings we have made, come to our aid. No good effort is ever lost. As one teacher has put it, "If I have enough on deposit in God's bank of good, He will honor my check of need. If I am overdrawn, I will start over and square my accounts."

Inner Peace

Men have found personal peace in every condition of life. Perhaps this is the Creative Principle's way of intimating to us the possibility of peace on a greater scale. In this age of worldwide communication we are conscious as it was never before possible to be conscious of the world condition; the hopes and despairs of other peoples in other lands—and of our land—their courage and their needs. The terrible waste and horror of war can no longer be glossed over by the martial music, the citations of valor, the spit and polish of military garb. Either as armchair travelers or actual visitors to faraway places we have looked into the faces of people whose eyes have a different slant, whose skin color is another shade, whose customs and cultures vary from our own—and have sensed our oneness beneath these outward variables. Their intelligence, their pride, their attainments, their shortcomings and weaknesses too, are our own, seen in another flesh disguise.

Modern technology has brought the whole world,

in all its grandeur and all its terror, right into our living rooms.

Seen in succession on our television screens men walking on the moon, and men being mutilated and slain "before our very eyes." We have witnessed the heights and the depths of the human predicament; the demand of the Spirit within us that we reconcile the dual aspects of our own nature, and the duality of our relationship to other people, other nations.

Never have the hazards of human relationships seemed so great, never the possibilities of the human potential so illimitable.

We can send men to the moon and back again, but we have not yet demonstrated the ability to live together in a community, or a community of nations.

Can there be peace in our time? O, yes, there can! Will there be peace in our time? Probably throughout the so-called civilized world there are very few persons who do not have "the will to peace," albeit on their own terms. Through what person, what group or nation, peace will come, only a very daring prophet would attempt to say.

The worldly wise, the statesmen, the diplomats, the military forces have tried every human method known to man. But there have been few treaties that have not been broken, and no force of arms applied against a resistant populace has ever brought security or lasting peace. Even force applied in defense of a righteous cause falls short of the ideal of enlightened men coming together in reason and tolerance to ameliorate differences, harmonize opposing views.

From the dawn of history men have gone to war, invoking the help of whatever gods they knew, praying that some higher power would be with them, to prosper their undertaking. All have prayed that God be on their side. Have any ever prayed that they be on God's side?

In this sophisticated age it is often remarked that God is always on the side of the forces that have the biggest guns, the mightiest armies. Yet there are instances, difficult to shrug off as chance or coincidence or luck, where apparently some higher Power has intervened in favor of the greater cause. In such instances He may make use of human agencies, without being limited by them, and sometimes He appears to act independently, in unforeseeable ways.

His appearance has taken many forms in history.

Divine Intervention?

Beleaguered Britain (believed by many to be descended from the Lost Tribes of Israel) was in the spring of the year 1588 assailed by the great host of the Spanish Armada. At a point when the British ships and forces were greatly outnumbered, their men and ammunition both exhausted, and defeat seemed inescapable, there came a sudden shifting of the wind that forestalled the advance of the Spanish fleet and enabled civilians from the English coastal villages to man their little boats and, under cover of darkness, rescue their helpless forces.

Centuries before that the land of Judah was attacked by the Moabites, the Ammonites, and men of Mount Seir—tribes that had been spared by the Israelites at the time they left Egypt—and they greatly outnumbered the men of Judah. Jehoshaphat was Judah's king, and he earnestly sought how to meet this invasion. He called the people together, proclaimed a fast, and prayed with them for divine guidance. "And the Spirit of the Lord came upon

Jahaziel . . . a Levite . . . and he said, 'Fear not, and be not dismayed at this great multitude; for the battle is not yours, but God's . . . Tomorrow go out against them, and the Lord will be with you.' "

So they arose early and went out toward the wilderness of Tekoa, and Jehoshaphat appointed singers to the Lord, praising Him "for his steadfast love endures for ever," and going before the army. Meanwhile the men of Ammon and Moab began fighting with the men of Mount Seir, so that by the time Judah arrived at the watchtower in the wilderness, the field was strewn with dead bodies, leaving cattle and clothing and other valuables which it took the men of Judah three days to transport back home with them.

So those who wanted peace and guidance and singing got these. Those who wanted strife and annihilation got death and destruction!

During World War II, an officer of the Allied forces was encamped near Michmash, about nine Roman miles north of Jerusalem and east of Beth-aven, opposed by enemy forces which were more numerous than his own. In his mental efforts, trying to determine a course of action, he was struck by the familiarity of the name *Michmash.* Was it not Biblical in origin? He got out his Bible and turned to I Samuel, Chapter 13. There, sure enough, was the account of how Saul in a similar situation had employed a clever stratagem to defeat the enemy. The Allied officer applied the same strategy with success, some three thousand years after the time of Saul!

In American history the praying founders experienced many instances of the apparent intervention of God in the country's destiny—of which Washington's leadership of his forces at Valley Forge is a striking example.

Coincidence, Chance?

Will the doubters say that God had no part in these things? That it was not God but a chance shifting of the winds, aided by the courage of the Britains who went out in the little boats from Dunkirk, that saved the British forces? That it was the impatience of the attackers in the wilderness that favored the men of Judah? That it was an officer's good memory that won victory at Michmash? And the intemperance of the Redcoats at Valley Forge that gave victory to Washington and the Colonial forces?

Assume, O doubter, that the Creative Principle of being did intervene in these encounters; what form would you expect the intervention to assume? Would God, like a vaudeville magician, wave a magic wand that would strike the aggressors dead? Or would He make use of the forces of nature and the nature of men to accomplish His will? This brings to mind a passage from Luke: "When Jesus perceived their questionings, he answered them, 'Why do you question in your hearts? Which is easier, to say, "Your sins are forgiven you," or to say, "Rise and walk"?' "

In the present time we see troubles on every hand, wars and rumors of wars, nation rising against nation, famines and earthquakes in various parts of the world; but this is not the end of the world. It may well be the darkness that precedes the dawning of a new age.

Beneath all the tumult and confusion there is a strong undercurrent of assurance that God is a very present help. In returning to the conscious realization of His presence and power, and our willingness to be guided by Him, shall peace and freedom be found.

The days of conquest by armed forces are numbered. Brute force is being superseded by the conquest of men's minds. The mightiest physical forces are not the largest but the smallest, the forces of atomic energy. The curious mind of man probes ever deeper into the sources of life, at the center of which he will find the First Cause. The exploration of outer space is being followed by ventures into inner space. This trend is leading men as never before to explore the inward approach to problems and their solutions, beginning with meditation and prayer. Have not the most unselfish and altruistic minds of all ages begun their inventions, discoveries, and innovations in this way? For what is prayer but "the soul's sincere desire," the instinctive yearning and turning of the created to the Creative Principle within him, in quest of answers to human needs, the fulfillment of high purposes, the possibilities of the vast unknown?

The manna that fell from the heavens and nourished the Israelites in the wilderness was a little thing, "fine as hoarfrost on the ground."

The atom is a little thing.

Bacteria are little things.

Prayer is a little thing.

Yet "more things are wrought by prayer than this world dreams of," for it invokes spiritual guidance. It notably brings peace to the individual; it can bring peace to the world by serving as the channel through which life's finer forces can become manifest, as at Dunkirk, at Tekoa, at Michmash, at Valley Forge. Prayer opens ways where to human sense there may seem to be none.

As Charles Fillmore and other prophets of the

present and the past have assured us, a few persons, devout and righteous, in the faithful practice of prayer for peace may cause many to be saved from disaster.

From the folk tales of Abraham we have the story of the wickedness of Sodom and Gomorrah, of how Abraham remonstrated with God in prayer to save them. Would God spare the cities from destruction if he could find fifty righteous men in them? It finally came down to God's agreeing to accept even ten! No doubt this legend is mostly symbolical, but the message is plain. Even a few men, devout and righteous, may be the occasion for saving many. A few persons, devout and righteous, in the faithful practice of prayer for peace may cause many to be spared the destruction that threatens. It could be likened to a huge tapestry suspended against a wall, with prayer groups like the pins that fasten the corners. Two are not enough, or many across the top perhaps not enough. The fabric could bulge and sag. But many such pins checkerboarded across it could hold it firm and strong.

Or to use another figure of speech, the prayers of a single person may be likened to a tiny trickle in the vast realm of Universal Mind out of which all creation takes form. Add another person, and another, hundreds, thousands. Make the prayers earnest, persistent, regular, and undoubting. Soon the tiny trickle becomes a rivulet, the rivulet a stream, the stream a mighty river that can become the agency of Universal Mind in ameliorating dissension and strife, in establishing the thought of peace, the will to peace, ideas that evolve into inspired right action that bring about liberty, justice, understanding, and accord.

Prosperity

"Do not be anxious, saying, 'What shall we eat?' or 'What shall we drink?' or 'What shall we wear?' For the Gentiles seek all these things; and your heavenly Father knows that you need them all. But seek first his kingdom and his righteousness, and all these things shall be yours as well"–Matt. 6:31-33.

"In the great Mind of God there is no thought of lack, and such a thought has no rightful place in your mind. It is your birthright to be prosperous, regardless of who you are or where you may be"–Charles Fillmore.

The letter of the law was given by Moses; the spirit of the law was given by Jesus Christ.

"Under the Mosaic law, a tithe (tenth) was required as the Lord's portion. Throughout the Old Testament the tithe is mentioned as a reasonable and just return to the Lord in acknowledgment of Him as the Source of bounty. After Jacob's vision of the ladder with angels ascending and descending upon it, he set up a pillar and made a vow to the Lord, saying: 'Of all that thou givest me I will give the tenth to thee.' "

Jesus expressed the spirit of the law succinctly when He said, "You receive without pay, give without pay," and "Give, and it will be given to you; good measure, pressed down, shaken together, running over, will he put into your lap." "For the measure you give will be the measure you get back."

Obedience to the Mosaic statement of the law is good discipline. It reminds us of the Source of our blessings, and is what might be considered the minimum conformance to the rule that "as you sow, so shall you reap." The sagacious farmer does not sell all the yield of the harvest, but sets aside the first—and best—portion for replanting. The tithe is an application of this rule to supply in the many forms that it comes to us. We may accept it initially on trial, to test its value. We tend to continue and reach beyond it, in grateful acknowledgment to God who truly opens the very windows of heaven and pours us out such a blessing that there shall not be room enough to receive it.

So we come into the larger fulfillment of the law as stated and exemplified by Jesus Christ. The Mosaic law is not nullified, but rather amplified and complemented by the teaching of Jesus, as the New Testament does not do away with the Old but fulfills it, and as the spiritually perceptive man emerges from the materially oriented man. This emerging man does not conform to the law because he must but because he wants to do so. He is emerging from the narrow confines of the decree "You must" to the wider world of "You may." From "You are required to" to "You are privileged to." From the status of servant to that of son. From the love of law to the law of love. From the closed fist to open arms, rejoicing with God in His glorious creation, and acclaiming the illimitable good.

Consider the bounty of the creation; a million million stars flung with apparent abandon but absolute precision across the void of space! Everything is done on a lavish scale. A thousand acorns fall to the ground for every oak that grows.

God stretches a rainbow across the heavens to proclaim the end of the flood.

He paints the trees each autumn in brilliant hues; and nightly brings their colors to the skies at sundown.

He spreads a bounteous table across the earth.

He fills the seas with fishes.

He hides treasure beneath the earth; gold, jewels, coal, oil.

He covers the hillsides with trees and puts streams in the valleys.

On every hand the Creative Principle of being seems to be telling us that lack and limitation are no part of the natural order of things. Lavish abundance without stint or limit is the divine order.

Activity is natural to this divine order, lethargy is not; health is natural, disease is not; prosperity is natural, lack is not. To be prosperous is as natural as it is to be well. Interference with the divine order in the human organism manifests as illness. Interference with the divine order in human activity manifests as lack, deprivation. Good circulation is one of the requirements of health; good circulation is also a requirement of prosperity.

The free-flowing stream remains clear and sparkling. It readily frees itself of impurities. When its waters are diverted and the flow obstructed, they quickly become stagnant. They have been taken out of circulation. So it is with regard to prosperity, inspiring such an affirmative prayer as: "*I am an open channel through which the healing, prospering currents of God's life are now flowing. God is my life, God is my health, God is my supply. In God is my trust.*"

Three Fundamentals

There are three fundamentals to the manifestation of prosperity that all of us need to know, because everyone is subject to them. The first step is to give. The second is to receive. The third is to share and conserve.

If you seek improvement in finances, circumstances, human relationship, health, take your sense of need out of isolation. Agree that improvement is possible. As long as you say, "There's nothing that can be done. I've tried everything. Nothing works," you are interfering with the natural flow of good. You are blocking the channel. As in spiritual healing, so in "demonstrating" prosperity, agree that the Creative Principle pronounced everything good in the beginning; that this pronouncement has never been annuled; that wellbeing is in consonance with the divine order; that our part is to "roll away the stone" of doubt and unbelief, so that the good, the better, the best may emerge.

The action of the Creative Principle is the same in spiritual healing and prosperity. Health may be defined as prosperity of the human organism; prosperity as health in financial and related matters.

Center your attention, then, not on what you appear to lack, but on what you can do to clear the way for the more desirable condition. Again then, review the concept that like tends to produce like; "everything brings forth after its kind." Concentrate thoughts, feelings, words, actions on constructive projects. What you can conceive, you can achieve. When desire becomes conviction, results are well on the way.

Act out the constructive thoughts, feelings, and

words. Make room for prosperity. "Nature abhors a vacuum," declared Spinoza. Take the words to heart. Is your thought cluttered? Clear it. Is your environment cluttered? Clear that too. Look about you.

"When you are moving from one house to another, do not take anything with you that you do not use at least once a year, and not all of that," a well-known architect advises. The point is applicable to our project of making room for prosperity. Examine desk drawers, filing cabinets, clothes closets, garage, the attic too if there is one. Contribute usable garments, furniture, knickknacks to the Goodwill Industries or the Salvation Army, or to a church or school auxiliary.

Where to Look

The materially-minded man (he usually thinks of himself as being a practical man!) looks to results. The spiritually-minded man, or spiritually-aspiring man, looks to causes. You have to sow before you can reap. Everything works that way. Another aspect of the same rule is that you have to give before you can receive.

Although the atmosphere around you is full of air, you cannot get another breath until you give the one you have.

So give what you have, in as many ways as you can through as many channels as you can, in as many places as you can.

Give as you would receive; richly, freely, promptly, without thought of return. The Creative Principle of being will take care of the return, which often comes in the most unexpected ways and through the most unforeseen channels. You give on the one hand, and receive on the other. Do not let the one hand know what the other is doing. Give as the sun gives its light, as the Son gives His love, as the blossom gives its beauty and fragrance (even when there may be no one to observe it). In a word, give because it is the natural thing to do, in consonance with the nature and order of the universe.

Do not be concerned about whether the giving seems to be practical or appreciated. "I've worked my fingers to the bone" (for an unresponsive son or daughter, sister or brother, employer or friend) is erroneous thinking! Was it only for appreciation that you gave? Or for an advantage? Or for a need? And can such a gift rightly be called giving? Rather give, not for another's need only, but for your own soul's need. For it is from our own soul's need that we find the soul's supply. And it is in the measure of our giving that we establish the measure of what shall come to us in return. Come it will, but how and when is in the hands of the Eternal. There let it be.

Again, let us remember that though to Spirit results are instantaneous, to consciousness they are progressive. Be not anxious. Let patience have her perfect work. When you are tempted to be anxious, and cannot see how a need will be met, allow yourself the speculation, "I wonder what God is going to do about this!"

If you pray for rain, it is only common sense to carry an umbrella. We tend always to get what we ask for from life; and a most potent way of asking for anything is preparing for it. All our preparation is not a conscious project. The person who has an avid interest in art is not necessarily planning a career in art. The person whose immoderate appetites invite ill health is not usually consciously asking for sickness. Many of us, in some difficult experience, may have cried out, "What have I done that this should come upon me?" and would be quick to resent someone's saying, "You asked for it!" although the conclusion seems justified.

Where we are in consciousness in the present is a prophecy of where we will be in fact in the future, for all our life is an evolving of what is involved in our attitudes toward life.

This does not mean that we are to center our consciousness on specific outward goals. It means that we should be concerned with causes more than with results. What we are saying here regarding prosperity, Edward Carpenter has written eloquently about a related matter:

"Seek not the end of love in this act or that act—lest indeed it becomes the end;

"But seek this act and that act and thousands of acts whose end is love—

"So shalt thou at last create that which thou desirest;

"And then when these are all past and gone there shall remain to thee a great and immortal possession, which no man can take away."

Substitute the word *prosperity* for *love,* and there appears a formula, which might be paraphrased by the admonition, "Don't try to work the law to a certain end, but work with the law, and the right result—even better than human sense may perceive—will appear." Be concerned with initiating the proper causes, and results will take care of themselves.

Getting and Retaining

What we attain by a certain standard of thought, feeling, and attitude must be maintained by the same standard. "Let us not grow weary in well-doing." And in whatever we wish to attain we must begin with what we have, and where we are.

In the story of Aladdin and the wonderful lamp, the genie did not appear simply because Aladdin wished him to appear. At first Aladdin did not know there was a genie. The genie appeared when Aladdin rubbed the lamp; in other words, when he set about putting into order what had been placed in his care.

Put your house—of possessions, as well as emotions—in order. "Rub your lamp!" Make the most and best of what you have, without deploring what you lack.

It is notable in the miracle stories of the Old and New Testaments that simple everyday things, things that were right at hand, were made the basis of results that reached far beyond the expected.

Elisha called forth abundance to meet the widow's needs by using the little oil she had in the house as a beginning.

Gideon's tiny band of three hundred men put to rout the great host of the Midianites.

David slew the giant with a pebble hurled from a slingshot.

Jacob won a deferred dower from his father-in-law, Laban, by means of a few spotted willow sticks.

Jesus broke and shared the five loaves and two fishes to feed the five thousand.

He drew forth money from the fish's mouth to pay taxes to Rome.

He took simple, untrained men as His evangelists, and laid the foundation for a religion that has spread throughout the world.

God Opens Ways

From real life in the present day comes the eloquent testimony of a correspondent with one of the Unity editors, telling a story of almost miraculous deliverance from besetting problems, in which her closing words were, "God opens ways where to human sense there seems to be no way!" This is true. But it is not all of the Truth. For God also uses ways that are so familiar, so commonplace, so close at hand that they are overlooked or ignored. Jesus Himself was overlooked in His own home town, moving Nathanael to exclaim to Philip, "Can anything good come out of Nazareth?" And many a present-day young artist has had to seek recognition abroad before finding acceptance nearer by.

So "What have you done with what you have?" is a question whose answer may reveal unrecognized possibilities. And for every blessing received there is a responsibility incurred.

Giving, of talents, abilities, attention, interest, love, service, opens the way for blessings to return to us through countless channels, and in both expected and unexpected ways. Being a good receiver of proffered blessings is as important as being a good giver: and it also involves new responsibilities. "If you have light, you must bear witness to the light," says Emerson. As you prosper, you have the responsibility of the wise and loving use of the bounties and opportunities that come to you. That is part of being a good receiver.

But there are other aspects to being a good receiver that relate more directly to the intangible forms of prosperity than to finances, possessions, and employment. To be a good receiver means to welcome new ideas, to be hospitable to strangers, newcomers, rivals, competitors, knowing that nothing and no one can take from you what by divine right belongs to you; and any of these apparent challenges to security may be blessings in disguise.

The person who interrupts you when you are working on some project may bring you an idea that helps the very project he has interrupted.

Being a good receiver means respecting and not violating a confidence someone has imposed on you.

It means letting a person know how much you appreciate a gift and/or his thoughtfulness in wanting to give it.

It means letting the other person have the spotlight, or his day in the sun, when you might have snatched it away; it means not spoiling the joke he is telling by anticipating the punch line, or by revealing the fact that you've heard it before, or maybe even told it to him originally.

It means rejoicing in another's good fortune as if it were your own.

Finally, being a good receiver means to be as steadfast in prayer, as unremitting in praise and gratitude in times of fulfillment, as in times of need, so that with Paul you can say, "I was not disobedient to the heavenly vision."

After Attainment

The third fundamental is largely a matter of integrity: What do we do after a desired form of affluence has been attained? Have we kept our promises? Rendered the best possible service? Fulfilled our obligations?

In the story of Elisha already referred to, the prophet's final admonition is, "Go, sell the oil and pay your debts, and you and your sons can live on the rest."

In times of distress we often make promises that are quickly forgotten or are brushed aside as being rash or extravagant, when the emergency is past. "I'd have a string of churches from one coast to the other if all the promises of building me a church—when the oil well comes in, or the mortgage is paid, or the afflicted member of the family is made well—were kept," declares a prominent minister.

He did not need a string of churches, or even one, as much as the troubled ones needed to fulfill their own assumed obligations. And the minister's place of ministry was built, in the financial sense, not by the fulfilled promises of a few, but by the not-very-promising small gifts of the many "little people," so-called, who gave richly of their modest means.

No manifestation of answered prayer, whatever its nature, is ever complete until thanks are offered to the Creative Principle who makes all good possible, and to the mundane channels that make the manifestation possible. Sometimes only worded thanks may seem sufficient, although the truly grateful heart usually finds something to do as well. The need to give thanks is as great as any need for which the thanks are given.

For every action there is a compensating and equivalent reaction; that is a law of physics and of metaphysics. We see it illustrated in the boomerang, in the Mosaic law of an eye for an eye and a tooth for a tooth, in the ebb and flow of the tides.

It exists, though we may not see it, as the law of karma, or cause and effect, in our individual life. The law exists, and it applies to all everywhere. We only determine our relationship to it.

Human Relations

"I know my own and my own know me"–John 10:15.

"See that none of you repays evil for evil . . . Do not quench the Spirit . . . but test everything; hold fast what is good"–I Thess. 5:15, 19, 21.

"Thou dost guide me with thy counsel"–Psalms 73:24.

"I do not love thee, Sabidius, nor can I say why; this only I can say, I do not love thee"–Martial.

"Have you not learned great lessons from those who reject you, and brace themselves against you? or who treat you with contempt, or dispute the passage with you?"–Walt Whitman.

Countless books have been written about the fine art of human relations, the art of getting along with people. But when it comes right down to individual cases, what is said in the books often seems not quite to apply to the situation at hand. Because no two human beings, no two situations, are ever quite the same. They are like a simple statement, which is like many other identical statements–except for dangling clauses, many modifiers. In human relationships there are dangling clauses, many modifiers. So in the final analysis you are faced by a circumstance, an encounter, an experience, that has never happened before.

Thank God, then, that you have an innate wisdom, an inner guide and counselor, which can be your very present help in the matter of human relationships as in other things. This does not mean that you should ignore all human and mundane channels of guidance to decision and action, but "do not be anxious how or what you are to answer or what you are to say; for the Holy Spirit will teach you in that very hour what you ought to say." Or as Emerson put it, "A man should learn to detect and watch that gleam of light which flashes across his mind from within, more than the lustre of the firmament of bards and sages."

Eternally you are a son of God and as such you are "the leading character in your own life's drama." One of the greatest factors in good human relationships is to recognize that everybody else is the leading character in his life's drama as well.

Because each of us is a son of God, and thereby unique, everything about us is of paramount interest and importance to us. We need to feel important, not in an egotistical sense, but in a truly appreciative sense, to bear witness to that nature in ourself and in others.

Personal Worlds

Each of us, no matter how much family we have, no matter how many friends and acquaintances we have, lives in a world of his own. It can be a very lonely world if we allow ourself to become too introspective, too much concerned with our own selfish though well-intentioned interests, too self-absorbed to realize and respond to the needs, the interests, the aspirations, the potentials in others.

When you are introduced to someone, do you pay attention to his name, or are you so absorbed in your own thoughts, or your concern about the impression you make, that you do not even hear his name? If you do not hear it clearly it may not be altogether your own fault, for names are not always clearly spoken, and if they are not familiar ones, may make no clear impression on you. Yet it is important that you should mentally register his name, for next to someone's actual person, his name is the most important thing about him—to him. Is this not true of you? On a printed page solidly covered with words, if your name appears even once among the hundreds of words before you, will your eyes not seek it out? If you are in a shop or a restaurant and the one who serves you calls you by name, does not his importance become greater in your estimation? "He called me by name!" He must be a superior person (or he makes you feel that you must be a superior person) to have recognized and remembered you.

If this is so for you, must it not be similarly so for others? You may think, as you meet someone for the first time, that you will probably never meet him again, do not particularly care whether you do; but that chance meeting might possibly become of great importance, and the more so if you take the trouble to ask him again to tell you his name, ask how it is spelled, repeat it if possible during subsequent conversation. He will know that you are a person worth knowing, because you have evinced an interest in what to him is as important as your name to you.

Perhaps the easiest thing to talk about, when you first meet someone, is yourself. You know more about yourself, is the ready excuse; but to the other person his own activities, his work, his family, his problems and achievements are paramount. Far from resenting questions you may ask, or remarks that invite him to tell about the trip he has made, the score he has made at golf, the attainments of his children, he almost invariably will respond warmly, and if you really listen and respond, you will have learned that there is a story in his life, and by extension in everyone's life.

Yes, there is a story in everyone's life, and though in some instances we are eager to know more about it, in others we could not care less. Why should this be so?

More Than Appears

We do not need to strain for ethereal explanations of our attraction to some persons and not toward others. There are logical and obvious reasons for many of them. We quickly discover kindred interests; or a person reminds us of someone we have known or liked; or our human shrewdness may nudge us toward developing an association that may be of material advantage to us. The authorative books on these subjects give us their reasons. Yet they do not seem to explain everything. The poet says,

"We live in deeds, not years; in thoughts, not
breaths;
In feelings, not in figures on a dial."

Why are we so drawn to some persons and not to others? Why do we accept some persons into our life at a first meeting as if they were old friends returned after long absence, and feel a sense of inner knowing that communicates without words, that is like resuming an interrupted friendship . . . or an interrupted relationship that has not reached fulfillment? There is something yet to be resolved. Some obligations to be fulfilled. Some debt to be repaid. Something we yet must do–or undo. Have we known them in some other time, some other life? Either this is so, or it is "as if" it were so.

You will not find this possibility presented in any book of modern psychology. It is a part of the ancient wisdom, and there are intimations of it even in the Gospels.

Obviously we are drawn to people with whom we have found or are finding interests in common. With some persons kindred interests and possibilities of friendship are immediately recognized; with others such discoveries must be sought out, and can be developed. Most of us actually are better in heart and spirit than we customarily reveal ourselves to be. It is rewarding to discover this "real self" in people. Eugene O'Neill once wrote a play in which all the characters wore masks that represented the way they wanted to appear to others, or perhaps the way they thought of themselves. Often when the mask was discarded the person back of it was different—better perhaps than the mask he wore.

In real life is this not almost literally true? Some of the masks may be worn to conceal sensitivities, or a sense of guilt, or of inadequacy.

Often when we do not like someone it is because secretly we feel he does not like us, or that we do not merit his approval or friendship. In such cases, we tend to disparage his actions, viewpoints, motives. The metaphysical way of improving such a relationship is to think of his talents, skills, accomplishments; and not only to think of them but to express this recognition to others. Perhaps each of us has at times felt a disapproval or bias against someone, only to learn that he has spoken of us in complimentary terms to someone else. It is very difficult to dislike someone who speaks well of you, if you feel that he is sincere and not merely voicing an affirmation.

Some psychologists tell us that if we generally do not like other people it is because we do not like ourself very well; that in the tendency to think and possibly speak disparagingly of others, we are actually trying to forgive ourself for our own shortcomings. We are saying to ourself: "See. You are not really so bad after all." This is a poor approach to a worthy attainment. We can do better by a different approach.

No matter how constructive we try to become, it is unlikely that we can honestly and sincerely like everyone equally well. The famous comedian who said he "never met a man he didn't like" either did not have a very keen sense of discrimination, or else he accepted people for what they truly are, and not for the varying degree in which they express what they are.

Some persons seem to have developed a special faculty for calling forth the best in others. Their talent takes many forms but even a cursory familiarity with these methods reveals that they have one thing in common. They are all based on recognizing some desirable trait or attribute in people, and contriving to let them know, without being too obvious, that it is recognized and appreciated.

Praise

The power of praise can scarcely be overrated, when it is honest and merited, and is not a euphemism for flattery. Flattery underestimates the intelligence and worth of its object. Praise is a recognition of merit, to which the so-called lower creation as well as human beings respond and thrive. The person with the proverbial "green thumb" is one who not only understands the kind of food, water, shade, and sunshine that his plants and grass and flowers need, but who loves them and even talks to them. Scientists have recently discovered and have been able to measure the reactions of plants to approval and praise on the one hand, threats and condemnation on the other. And everyone who has a pet bird or a four-footed friend can testify to the pet's sensitivity and response.

Businessmen have become millionaires by understanding and responding to mankind's need for recognition and appreciation. Adequate or even generous compensation for services rendered, along with gifts and bonuses, are not in themselves enough. The warm clasp of a hand, the intelligent acknowledgment of a special skill, invariably call forth greater achievements, deeper loyalty, than pay alone will do. The dignity of the human spirit demands recognition. Everyone is a unique creation, and no two of us have identical talents, skills, capabilities. Consequently all of us can learn from others. A successful leader of men never tells them that they are wrong. He recognizes their merits and appeals to their self-respect, their integrity, their pride in accomplishment. "No one works for me. Others work with me," is his attitude.

Do Not Judge Others

Ministers, doctors, social workers, personal counselors are most successful in helping others if they never indicate surprise or shock at the self-revelations of those who consult them. Their purpose is not to pass judgment, to deplore, to condemn, but to consider what seem to be the factors in the problem presented, what solutions are acceptable to the patient or counselee. The counselor may believe that he has answers that are superior to those that the patient can accept, but the counselor's problem is to help the patient find the answers that he can live with most comfortably. And not infrequently what the patient needs is not some prescription or profound advice, not to be either praised for his successes and virtues or condemned for his shortcomings, but to be understood.

The Power That Attracts

A minister who was attending a convention entered a lounge in the hotel where the convention was held. Delighted to see some of his fellow ministers sitting around a table, he was dismayed by the sudden silence that fell upon the group as he approached. One of the younger of the group broke the silence by explaining, "We were just talking about you when you somewhat startled us by suddenly appearing in the doorway."

"That's interesting," the newcomer remarked. "What did you find interesting to talk about?"

"We were puzzled about why it is that wherever you go, you always attract such a large congregation."

"That has puzzled a good many people. I sometimes wonder about it myself."

"I think I know the answer," the young minister volunteered.

"What do you think it is?" the newcomer invited.

"I think it is not your brilliance, or oratory, or anything like that—"

"I don't have much of those qualities!"

"—it is simply that you love people!"

Never underestimate the power of unselfish love.

The instructor in a ministerial training school once told his students, referring to a well-known minister: "If you want an example of a man who has made a successful career out of just one idea, I can name you one. No matter what his subject is, it always turns out to be love."

It would be difficult to choose any one subject as the theme for a lifetime career that could equal love.

It has to be genuine.

There are many counterfeits, many pretenders to that throne. Possessiveness is one. So are self-interest, and sentimentality, and domination ("I am only doing this because I love you and want to save you from getting hurt"). The innate within us senses these shams, and if we live close enough to it, we avoid being deceived by what may even be unconscious or unintended deceptions.

There is a difference between loving and liking, too. A missionary returning to this country from Asia was asked how he felt about the soldiers of a warring country where he tried to serve young people especially. He seemed lost in thought for a few moments before he spoke. Finally he answered, "I love them, but I do not like them." He loved the sinners but did not like the things with which they identified themselves.

Become Involved

Most of us grow most and develop fastest when we permit ourselves to associate with persons of varied cultures and points of view. We may not like to have our pet notions challenged at the time this occurs, but we may come to cherish most those who have, as Walt Whitman put it, "disputed the passage" with us.

Perhaps each of us numbers among his acquaintances at least one person who states his opinions as if they were incontrovertible facts. Mentally his stance may be almost that of a boxer preparing to fend off a blow. If instead of defending an opposing opinion you respond with the assertion, "You are absolutely right—from your point of view!" you may see a look of surprise come over his features, as if he was suddenly made to realize that there were (or at least might be) other points of view worth considering.

Everyone is right from his own point of view. If he were not, would he not change? It would seem so, and yet it is not always so. It is only since men have flown to the moon and back, and photographed the "good green earth" in its roundness, that the leader of the cult which had always maintained that the earth is flat (despite all contrary evidence) has conceded that it must indeed be round. And there are some who would agree with the response of the octogenarian who for the first time heard the theory of evolution expounded: "If it is so, I hope people never find it out!" The adjustment to so great a change of belief seemed just too much.

There is a point here for all aspiring Truth-seekers. Keep flexible in thought and emotion. The young tree is seldom damaged by assailing winds. Its trunk and limbs are pliable. The old trees whose branches have become stiff and brittle suffer the most. They can no longer adjust. So although we must perforce grow along with the years, we do not want to become inflexible, so fixed in our thought about "the way things have always been done" that we have closed minds.

We Are Not Alone

We do not have to be in the category of minister,

doctor, counselor to apply these concepts in everyday living. Some of us have wider circles of influence than others; many of us have more influence on other persons than we know or recognize. In person, by telephone, letter, or other means of communication we touch the lives of other people every day, many times a day. Knowingly or otherwise, we exert a certain influence upon the physical, mental, and emotional atmosphere of others, and they upon us. No one lives to himself alone, however it may seem to be.

To human sense we are all separate and apart from one another. We signal across to one another by thought, word, action. We strive to communicate by these more-or-less outward means; but Truth reveals a deeper and more subtle, surer way of communication. When in meditation and prayer we reach toward the center of being—the center of life, light, and love within us—we are coming closer to the center of being in others. We reach past any tendency to dominate, to exert human will or mind power over others, or such possible tendencies in others. Reaching to the Creative Principle, the Christ nature in us greets the Christ nature in others. We salute the innate nature, prophetic of the fulfillment of Jesus' words when He said, "I in them and thou in me, that they may become perfectly one."

Says Charles Fillmore: "The mind of man is like a clear stream that flows from some lofty mountain. It has nothing at its point of origin to disrupt or distort it, but as it flows out into the plain of experience, it meets the obstruction of doubt and fear. It is here that dams are built and its course is turned in many ways.

"Whoever formulates a creed or writes a book,

claiming it to be an infallible guide for mankind; whoever organizes a church in which it is attempted, by rules and tenets, to save men from their evil ways; whoever attempts to offer, in any way, a substitute for the one omnipresent Spirit of God dwelling in each of us, is an obstructor of the soul's progress."

A Man, A Tree, A River

Let us say, and seek to make our words as true in fact as they are in principle: "Father, I should like to be like a tree, firmly rooted in the good earth, but reaching always heavenward, facing the smiles of summer and the frowns of winter with boughs that bend with the breezes, but do not break before them; sending my roots ever deeper into the rich moist soil, and my branches higher and higher into the vibrant blue; giving shelter to songbirds and sustenance to the small creatures that live tremulously about my roots; sending forth young green shoots and branches like curious venturesome new thoughts, and not fearing to drop off old branches that have served their purpose; growing with the years—not knotted and gnarled and crooked, but straight and strong and upright.

"Or let me be like a river whose waters find their source in the rains of heaven, and whose destiny is the illimitable ocean; a river beneath whose eddying surface still swift waters run to join their parent sea, unstayed by obstacles, patiently and persistently going over, under, around them, in season calm, in season gay, ever going onward; bringing refreshment and supply to multitudes, carrying cargoes of plenty and pleasure, forceful at floodtime yet faithful in drought; remembering always that though my way be devious and winding over rocks and waste places, that my source is God's heavens and my goal His boundless sea.

"But God, I thank Thee that I am man, embodying the tree and the stream, fixed and deep-rooted in consciousness of my true nature and purpose, immovable in a knowledge of Truth, yet growing into ever-broadening understanding of Your boundless sea of wisdom, adapting to flood and drought, the breeze and tempest, yielding to their moods yet ungoverned by them, dropping dead branches of thought like the tree, clearing away debris like the stream, and like both of them fulfilling life's purpose, unthwarted by circumstance, reaching ever upward and forward because—I am a man."

Twelve and One

"In the new world, when the Son of man shall sit on his glorious throne, you who have followed me will also sit on twelve thrones, judging the twelve tribes of Israel. And every one who has left houses or brothers or sisters or father or mother or children or lands, for my name's sake, will receive a hundredfold, and inherit eternal life. But many that are first will be last, and the last first"–Matt. 19:28-30.

Any serious student of spiritual things who is not bound to some dogmatic form of faith must have observed that the story of Jesus conforms to a cosmic pattern. Astrologers relate His life to that of "the enthroned Sun-God and his twelve powers." "All the eastern nations," says Origenes, "the people of India, the Persians, conceal sacred mysteries under their religious myths; the sages and philosophers of all religions penetrate the true meaning, while the ignorant see only the exterior symbol–the bark that covers it." James Morgan Pryse relates the story to the symbolic drama of the Lesser Mysteries of the ancient Greek religion. Charles Fillmore writes, "Jesus was the star actor in the greatest drama ever played on earth. This drama was developed in the celestial realm, its object being to inject new life into perishing man. The full significance of this great plan of salvation cannot be understood by man until he awakens faculties that relate him to the earth beneath and the heavens above."

What does this do to the faith of the follower of

traditional religious faith, Christian, Jew, Buddhist? Must they cry, "They have taken away my Lord," as if Moses and Jacob (whose name was changed to Israel) and Siddhartha Gautauma (who became the Buddha) and Jesus (who became the Christ) never really lived at all, but were only symbolic portrayals of mental and emotional states of consciousness?

Or might the devout believers be justified in pointing to all these parallels as evidence of a grand cosmic design? The ancient followers of the Hermetic philosophy have contributed a saying which is as valid today as it was in the time of Hermes the Thrice-Great, who declared: "As within, so without; as above so below." Or as Emerson put it, "The microcosm and the macrocosm are the same. The world globes itself in a drop of dew."

It might be said that if the cynics could be proved right the world would be the poorer for it, because mankind needs the assurance—at the present time in the world's history more than ever—that there have been those who have not only glimpsed a vision of things transcendent, but have actually lived them, and like fabled Prometheus brought the fire of heaven down to earth to warm the hearts and lives of men.

So do men reason and ponder.

The practical man will take the truth where he finds it, and put it to use in his personal life. And this is where the concept of Jesus and His disciples and the mystery of "the twelve thrones" can be of pragmatic value. For the story of Jesus and His calling of the Twelve, Buddha and his twelve faithful ones, Israel and his twelve sons who became the founders of the twelve tribes, all find a parallel in the story of individual man, finding dominion over his own forces of body, mind, and soul; marshaling his twelve mind powers to unified activity in his personal world.

Twelve seems to represent a pattern of completion. We see it represented on the face of our clocks in the twelve hours of the dial, in the twelve months of the year, the twelve signs of the zodiac, the duodecimal system of ancient Egypt, the twelve inches to the foot, the twelve labors of Hercules, the twelve foundations and twelve gates of the Holy City, the twelve gems in the breastplates of the Jewish priests.

In the human organism, man is conceived to have basically twelve powers or faculties of mind, which may be related to twelve nerve centers in the human body. Charles Fillmore and certain leaders in other forms of philosophic faith—notably the so-called biochemists—are quite specific about this. For the average (and even quite above-average) student, experience suggests that it is the part of wisdom to center one's attention on the qualities of mind, and let the innate Creative Principle direct their energies, as in the case of the circulation of the blood, the digestion of food, and other involuntary actions of the mind, rather than upon corresponding parts of the body.

When we recognize these twelve powers and seek to bring them into harmonious coordination, it is like Jesus calling His twelve disciples, according to Charles Fillmore. He relates each of the twelve powers to one of the twelve disciples.

Here, then, is a list of the twelve disciples, the related powers of mind, and the nerve and gland centers in the body:

Peter—Faith—the center of the brain, or pineal gland.

Andrew—Strength—the small of the back.
James, son of Zebedee—Judgment—pit of the stomach.
John—Love—back of the heart.
Philip—Power—the root of the tongue.
Bartholomew—Imagination—between the eyes.
Thomas—Understanding—the front brain.
Matthew—Will—the forehead, above the eyes.
James, son of Alphaeus—Order—back of the navel.
Simon, the Cananaean—Zeal—base of the brain.
Thaddaeus—Elimination—the lower back.
Judas Iscariot—Life Conserver—generative center.

Peter

If Peter were here today he would be known as Simon Johnson, for when he first encountered Jesus he was known as Simon Bar-jona—that is, Simon, son of John. Jesus gave him a new name partly playfully, partly affirmatively, for He said, "And I tell you, you are Peter, and on this rock I will build my church, and the powers of death shall not prevail against it." Peter (from the Greek *Petros*) means rock; and it is significant that this statement came just on the heels of Simon's discernment that Jesus was the very embodiment of the Christ Spirit. This—the embodiment of the Christ Spirit—is the rock on which His church must be built.

For Peter, at this stage of his development, eager and impetuous as he was, lacked the steadfastness on which to build anything enduring. He was far from a rock, but more like a stone in the making. He was to fail time and again, as when he tried to walk on water, when he lopped off the ear of the arresting soldier in Gethsemane, when he vowed never to deny his Lord (and denied Him thrice). But he did not give up trying, so that finally, by the time of the Ascension, he was a veritable rock of Gibraltar. His preaching at Pentecost was so powerful that some three thousand souls were converted by his words and were baptized. He rapidly took the lead over all the other apostles, as recounted in the first twelve chapters of Acts, until the days of Paul's leadership.

There is a magnificent tribute to the power of faith in the eleventh chapter of the epistle to the Hebrews, which begins, "Now faith is the assurance of things hoped for, the conviction of things not seen."

It was Jesus who referred to this same endowment when He told Peter, "I will give you the keys to the kingdom of heaven, and whatever you bind [affirm] on earth shall be bound in heaven, and whatever you loose [deny] on earth shall be loosed in heaven." And in all His teaching, Jesus emphasized that the ruling forces of both heaven and earth are within man.

"If you have faith as a grain of mustard seed, you will say to this mountain, 'Move hence to yonder place,' and it will move; and nothing will be impossible to you."

Because a mustard seed is a very small seed, this passage has often been taken to mean that only a very small faith is required. And truly, even a very small faith will do very much more than no faith at all. But the significance of Jesus' allusion is quite different.

What *is* the faith of the mustard seed?

It has the faith to *become* a mustard plant! In Palestine where Jesus lived, He had no doubt many times marveled at the mustard plant that could spring from so small a seed, a plant tall enough, so one commentator affirms, to shield a horse and rider from the sun.

The faith that moves mountains of difficulty is the faith to become the Christ-filled man that He told us about, and in His person exemplified—the emerging man of the second coming.

Andrew

"When a strong man, fully armed, guards his own palace, his goods are in peace," said Jesus.

Andrew is the strong man among the twelve. The Greek meaning of Andrew is "strong man."

"Andrew, his brother." In three out of the four gospels that is the way Andrew is referred to—as the brother of Peter. That is about the only way anybody thinks of Andrew. And yet if it had not been for Andrew we might never have heard of Peter, and Peter might never have heard of Jesus.

"He first found his brother Simon," and hastened to tell him that he had found the Christ. Through all the days of the journeys with Jesus we know Andrew only as the disciple who helped people to find each other.

It must have been a little hard to take at times, playing the role of the man who seemed always to walk in the shadow of a greater. Yet the same spirit rested upon and dwelt in Andrew as in his brother, and in whatever Peter accomplished—which was much—Andrew perforce had a share.

We have no record that Andrew ever preached a sermon, or healed the sick, or raised the dead, or cast out demons. He worked no miracles, wrote no letters, proclaimed no visions. He simply brought people together, and mostly he brought them to Christ. He began close at hand, with his brother, which is a hard place to begin, but a logical one.

It was Andrew who brought a little boy to Jesus on that day when the five thousand assembled to hear Jesus speaking from the hillside near Capernaum, and they became so enrapt with the magic of His words that they forgot all about mealtime (no mean miracle in its own right). "There is a lad here who has five barley loaves and two fish; but what are they among so many?" It was, of course, Andrew, "Simon Peter's brother," who brought the report and the lad to Jesus.

It was Andrew who brought men from other lands to the Master. And if bringing youth to Him makes Andrew a kind of apostle of youth, it might be said that bringing foreigners to Him makes him father of the missionary movement. "Among those who went up to worship at the feast were some Greeks. So these came to Philip, who was from Bethsaida in Galilee, and said to him, 'Sir, we wish to see Jesus.' Philip went and told Andrew; Andrew went with Philip and they told Jesus."

Andrew exemplifies Proverbs 18:10: "The name of the Lord is a strong tower." He had a kind of inward strength that always excites our admiration: the ability to let his works go before him, so that you see them rather than him. "I am strong in the Lord and in the power of His might" is an affirmation for those who seek to manifest more of their own Andrew-nature.

Andrew and Simon Johnson, the finder and the found, the introvert and the extrovert, the assertive leader and the power behind him! May their nature in us today help to lead us, and through us others, out of things that seem to separate us to those that unite us, for the crying need of this time—and of all time—is that we find that which is like Jesus in one another and in ourself.

James, Son of Thunder

Peter, James, and John, these three. How often we find them mentioned in that order! They were the members of the executive committee among the twelve, and as such were called upon to share both privileges and responsibilities unknown to the other nine.

James was to John, his brother, what Andrew was to his brother Peter. But James was included in the inner circle often where Andrew was not. He was with Jesus in the house of Jairus and witnessed the raising of his daughter from the dead. He was present on the Mount of Transfiguration when the face and vesture of the Master seemed to glow with an inner light, a crystalline quality so that His face "shone like the sun, and his garments became white as light."

He beheld the figures of Moses and Elijah, as they talked with Jesus, and he heard a voice say, "This is my beloved Son . . . listen to him." After the last supper with its tender message of communion, he accompanied his brother and Peter as they crossed the valley of Kedron and climbed the slope of the Mount of Olives to the Garden of Gethsemane, where Jesus withdrew a little way from them for prayer and meditation, in preparation for the epochal events to come. "My soul is very sorrowful, even to death; remain here, and watch with me." And as He rejoined them, and found them sleeping, "So, could you not watch with me one hour? . . . The spirit indeed is willing, but the flesh is weak."

James, like the rest of the disciples—and like us

modern disciples as well—had his weak points as well as his strong points. Mark tells us that Jesus surnamed him and his brother John "Boanerges" which means "sons of thunder." And not without reason, for when Jesus and some of the disciples on their way to Jerusalem entered a village of the Samaritans and were not welcomed, he and John were ready to burn the village down. Jesus rebuked them, "and they went on to another village." Again when the brothers came upon a man who in Jesus' name was casting out devils from troubled men, they forbade him because "he does not follow with us." Jesus' response was, "Do not forbid him; for he that is not against you is for you."

Do we not get the feeling that Jesus sets the disciples a personal standard, and then by His own experience and theirs calls forth in them the potentials that He discerns in them?

This is revealed even in His initial approach to them. Had He said to these rough fishermen, "Come, leave your trade, and I will make religious evangelists out of you," would they have left their nets as readily? But He talked in their own metier: "I will make you fishers of men." And He did.

The writer, A. Milton Smith, states that it has been said of James that "Since he was older than John and more deliberate than Simon Peter, his judgment may have been depended on more than theirs."

Charles Fillmore relates James to the quality of judgment. "Wisdom," he says, "includes judgment, discrimination, intuition," and that the house or throne of this wise judge is the solar plexus or pit of the stomach.

"Fishers of men." James not the least, for he did indeed develop wisdom and judgment, in the strenuous years following Pentecost; a leader in the church; a man of strong opinions, but judgment that must be respected; nothing lukewarm (that word has a Scriptural origin, too) about him. Nothing indifferent. No question where he stood. No trimming of his sails to winds of expediency. He was forthright, vigorous, and perhaps the quality that made him a "son of thunder" also made him the church's first martyr.

John, the Beloved

John was the disciple "whom Jesus loved." He writes of himself: "One of his disciples, whom Jesus loved, was lying close to the breast of Jesus" at the last supper. It was at Peter's instigation that he asked Jesus which of the twelve was to betray Him. John was the youngest of the twelve and at this point he deserved the name that Jesus gave to him and James, "sons of thunder." The brothers started out very much alike; they shared the same ambitions, and felt that they should be the ones to sit at the left and right of the Master when He should come into His kingdom; they were filled with wrath at the villagers in Samaria who denied them lodging; they were closer than many brothers. Where there was one, the other was likely to be close by. But people can change and mellow . . . as, for instance, the bishop of a modern church, counseling a young man about his emotional drive. The bishop seemed so understanding of his problems, so sympathetic in his response, that finally the young man dared to ask, "How is it that you, a bishop of the church, can be so understanding of my problems?" "Well, you see, Son," the bishop responded, "I haven't always been a bishop!"

Today, as we think of James, who became a kind

of elderly statesman, characterized by tolerance and good judgment, and of John whom Jesus loved, and who wrote the Gospel that bears his name and probably the three Epistles of John and The Revelation, it seems incredible that they ever could have been as bold and brash and self-serving as they were when Jesus called them from their trade to become fishers of men.

The Gospel of John presents Jesus in a very different manner than the writers of the first three Gospels do. In it we see a perception of the true nature of Jesus Christ and His mission. The fourteenth through seventeenth chapters are among the most beautiful, comforting, and inspiring in the entire Bible; the book of Revelation is the most mystical.

Reasons for identifying this disciple with the attributes of love, and with the heart in man's personal world of body, needs little amplification. Next to Jesus Himself, John in his maturity comes closest to exemplifying the Christ Spirit in mankind; so much so that we might well feel that when we can embody this spirit in its fullness, all else will fall into line. For as a man thinks in his heart—that is, with deep feeling—so he will become, and out of the heart proceed the issues of life.

Philip

"Among the disciples of Jesus Christ, Philip represents the power faculty of the mind. The word *Philip* means 'a lover of horses.' In physical activity the horse represents power; the ox, strength. Each of the twelve fundamental faculties of man has an ego that reflects, in a measure, the original man idea of God. In the body consciousness the twelve disciples, as egos, have twelve centers, or thrones, from which they exercise their power . . . Power is one branch of the great tree; in Genesis it is named 'life.' The body of the life tree is the spinal cord, over which the motor system, with branches to every part of the organism, exercises its nervous energy." So writes Charles Fillmore.

What do we know of Philip as a man?

Andrew found Peter, and Philip found Nathanael (Bartholomew), but Jesus found Philip and said, "Follow me." Philip, John tells us, was from Bethsaida, the home of Andrew and Peter. He may have heard about Jesus from them.

It is only in the fourth Gospel that we learn anything about Philip. There four incidents are related. The first was when Jesus found and called him. The second was at the feeding of the five thousand, when "the twelve came and said to him, 'Send the crowd away, to go into the villages and country round about, to lodge and get provisions, for we are here in a lonely place.' And Jesus responded, 'You give them something to eat.' " John tells us that Jesus said to Philip, " 'How are we to buy bread, so that these people may eat?' This he said to test him, for he himself knew what he would do. Philip answered him, 'Two hundred denarii would not buy enough bread for each of them to get a little.' " Then Jesus demonstrated "the sufficiency of God" by the miracle of increase in which all were fed. Why did Jesus ask Philip instead of Matthew, for instance, who was well acquainted with money matters, or Judas, who was the treasurer for the twelve? If Philip was to activate the *power* of the twelve, was not Jesus perhaps preparing him for this?

The third instance is when Greeks came to worship at the feast of the Passover. "So these came to Philip, who was from Bethsaida in Galilee, and said to him, 'Sir, we wish to see Jesus.' Philip went and told Andrew; Andrew went with Philip and told Jesus." Why does John remind us of Philip's home town? Was it that the Greeks were also from there?

We begin to see a pattern. Andrew, who is related to the quality of strength, and Philip to the quality of power, have a common work to do of bringing people (qualities of mind) together. They appear to work so quietly that their significance is almost missed. It develops later. Philip particularly, it might be said, is a "late bloomer." It is not until after Jesus' resurrection that he appears to have "come into his own."

The fourth glimpse of him is at the last supper. Simon Peter and Thomas, perplexed by the turn events have taken, voiced their confusions in the questions they asked Jesus. Philip's question was the final one. " 'Lord, show us the Father, and we shall be satisfied.' Jesus said to him, 'Have I been with you so long, and yet you do not know me, Philip? He who has seen me has seen the father; how can you say, "Show me the Father"? Do you not believe that I am in the Father and the Father in me?' "

Every man must mold the forces of his own being, as Jesus molded the twelve who were like parts of His own being. God gives us the essentials. As Emerson has put it, "What we are is God's gift to us; what we become is our gift to Him."

Philip was one of the eleven when, after the resurrection, He appeared to them. His words, "Behold, I send the promise of my Father upon you; but stay in the city, until you are clothed with power from on high," might have been especially for Philip; at the very least, he would claim them for his own.

Nathanael Bartholomew

Nathanael and Bartholomew are the same person. To the writers of the synoptic gospels he was Bartholomew; to John he was Nathanael. Peter was first called Simon Bar-jonah, which is to say, Simon, son of Jonah. Nathanael was the son of Tolomai: thus, Nathanael Bar-Tolomai. He was the friend whom Philip brought to Jesus after Jesus had called Philip with the words: "We have found him of whom Moses in the law and also the prophets wrote, Jesus of Nazareth, the son of Joseph." And Philip responded, "Come and see." When Jesus saw Nathanael approaching, He said, "Behold, an Israelite indeed, in whom is no guile!"

"How do you know me?" Nathanael exclaimed.

"Before Philip called you, when you were under the fig tree I saw you."

"Rabbi, you are the Son of God! You are the King of Israel!"

"Because I said to you, I saw you under the fig tree, do you believe? You shall see greater things than these . . . Truly, truly, I say to you, you will see heaven open, and the angels of God ascending and descending upon the Son of man."

In these few words are told most of the things we know about Nathanael as a man. Add to this only that he was born in Cana of Galilee, the place of Jesus' first miracle.

But the words of Jesus seem to confirm that he may well be made a fitting symbol for the quality of imagination in us all, for Jesus' words about seeing the angels ascending and descending upon the Son of man certainly indicate that He saw in Nathanael the capacity for spiritual insight, which is perhaps the very highest form of imagination.

The implication here is that Jesus experienced a kind of prevision regarding Nathanael and the fig tree, a form of extrasensory perception which in the present day is coming up for thoughtful consideration not only by persons of a superstitious and fanatical turn of mind but by profound and serious thinkers. For what we call constructive imagination may sometimes be an instance of extrasensory perception.

"The Spirit of truth projects into the chambers of imagery pictures that, rightly understood, will be a sure guide for all people who believe in the omnipresence of mind," writes Charles Fillmore. By "chambers of imagery" he is of course alluding to Ezekiel 8:12, which in the Authorized Version reads, "Son of man, hast thou seen what the ancients of the house of Israel do in the dark, every man in the chambers of his imagery?" The Revised Standard Version makes "chambers of imagery" read "room of pictures," more literal perhaps, but we surmise that Nathanael Bar-Tolomai would have preferred the older version.

"Where there is no vision, the people perish: but he that keepeth the law (of vision), happy is he." Or, "Where there is no prophecy the people cast off restraint, but blessed is he who keeps the law."

Thomas

How curious, anyone might say, that Thomas, whom we always have called "doubting Thomas," should be compared to the quality of understanding: yet "doubt," said the Poughkeepsie seer, Andrew Jackson Davis, "is the beginning of wisdom." Perhaps he meant that if you doubt enough you will investigate, you will ask questions, you will seek knowledge, and so come into understanding. For the poet cries:

"Oh, what dusty answers gets the soul,
When hot for certainties in this our life!"

Thomas was not a mystic but a realist. He looked through dark glasses. But we must remember that not only he but all the disciples were faced with an experience, an association, that was unique, unprecedented.

Jesus Christ did not speak as the scribes and Pharisees, but as one having an inner authority; an authority that the twelve all recognized or they never would have left their habitual occupations to follow Him. Perhaps sometimes they wondered why they had done so! He did not act from the motives that activated most men. Almost everything He said and did was at variance with the mores of the time—even of this present time.

So it is not difficult for us to say, "There but for the grace of God go I!" as we consider their reactions.

We are trying to think in terms of a transcendent spirit, the spirit of Jesus Christ. We are trying to relate characteristics of avowedly historical personalities to phases of our own individual life. We are doing this from afar, in the light—and possible darkness—of twenty centuries of time and a world of difference in customs and cultures—with only the printed word, an empathy with the dual nature of man, and the light of inspiration to guide us.

They were faced with the immediacy of an involving experience.

As in the case of Philip, what little we know about Thomas is to be gleaned from the gospel of John.

We do not know how or where Thomas met Jesus. We do not know whence he came, anything about his background except that he was a twin. His other name, Didymus, means "twin."

He was with Jesus at the raising of Lazarus. He knew the feelings of the Jews toward Jesus, and said to the other disciples, "Let us also go, that we may die with him."

At the Last Supper, he was the one who said, in response to Jesus' assurance that He was going to prepare a place for them, "Lord, we do not know where you are going; how can we know the way?"

He was absent when after the resurrection Jesus appeared amongst the disciples, who told Thomas, "We have seen the Lord"; to which Thomas gave the famous answer, "Unless I see in his hands the print of the nails, and place my finger in the mark of the nails, and place my hand in his side, I will not believe." It was eight days later when Jesus again appeared amongst them, and said to Thomas, " 'Put your finger here, and see my hands; and put out your hand, and place it in my side; do not be faithless, but believing.' Thomas answered him, 'My Lord and My God!' Jesus said to him, 'Have you believed because you have seen me? Blessed are those who have not seen and yet believe.' "

By our very incarnation in this world of objectivity, we have demanded to learn by experience. At times it is a hard way though a very thorough one, for if the Lord of our own being demands that we see "the print of the nails," we are in a sense asking for them to appear in ourself. But if we can reach a state of consciousness where we can believe without seeing, Thomas has done a good work in our inner nature, enabling us to echo his words, "My Lord and

My God!" How much like flowers we are!

Matthew, Man of Means

Luke called him Levi in the Book of Acts, and Matthew in his gospel narrative. Most of us probably think of him as Matthew because of the Gospel bearing that name, rather than Levi.

Jesus saw him at the receipt of customs. "Follow me," said Jesus, and as fishermen had left their nets at His word, so Matthew, the publican, left his station without question or delay. The gospels do not tell us what led up to his conversion. But he was from Capernaum, where Jesus did many of His mightiest works. It was there that the palsied man was cured, the lepers healed, the demoniac freed of his obsessing devil, the blind man made to see, the daughter of Jairus, ruler of the synagogue, raised to life.

He could scarcely have failed to know of these wonders in a time and area where news traveled fast—not by the printed word, radio, or television, all still far-off in time—but by word of mouth. Had he witnessed a healing, conversed with some of those whose life Jesus had touched? Had Peter, James, or John, who had left their nets at His word, inspired his response? Conjectural, but perhaps justifiable conclusions.

Soon after the call, Matthew celebrated with a feast. Luke tells about it: "And Levi made him a great feast in his house; and there was a large company of tax collectors and others sitting at table with them. And the Pharisees and their scribes murmured against his disciples, saying, 'Why do you eat and drink with tax collectors and sinners?' And Jesus answered them, 'Those who are well have no need of a physician, but those who are sick; I have not come to call the righteous, but sinners to repentance.' "

When something in us is touched by inspiration, there is the urge to share the word with others, as Matthew, by means of a feast, somewhat like a wake in memory of his past way of life, or like a wedding as he espouses the way of the Christ. "One loving spirit sets another heart on fire," writes T. R. Glover. We see this magic at work in Matthew and the others. We see how the Christ Spirit called to the divine potential in men of old. We feel its call in us today.

Matthew has been likened to the faculty of will. Man tends to go his own way, exercising his own will power according to his own understanding. He needs not less will, but guided will and understanding. Even Jesus Himself had to face this challenge. Man's insistence on having his own way, according to his own will has—despite all the advances in scientific knowledge, and philosophical cogitation—brought our human world to the verge of chaos. Many advanced thinkers believe that only a spiritual revival can prevent this. Charles Fillmore asserts that eons ago man lost conscious contact with God. Realization that to invite the will of God does not mean punishment, suffering, or retribution, but good and only good, is man's salvation. The will of God can never be less good than our will for ourselves and one another but better.

If there still lingers in our mind and heart a fear of invoking God's will, perhaps we can get around that fear, with another way of phrasing the thought: *"I invite the powerful, loving action of God in my life."*

James, Son of Alphaeus

There were three pairs of brothers among the Twelve. There were also three pairs who shared the same name, or at least part of a name: two named Judas, two named Simon, two named James. Of the two Jameses, we know best the James who was the brother of John. They were the sons of Zebedee. Of James, the son of Alphaeus, we wish we might know more. He is often called James the Less, meaning (partly) less prominent, of smaller stature. Some think he was the brother of Jesus, James the church moderator, and James the writer.

The names of the apostles are not always given in the same order, but they are always given in three groups of four each. Peter always heads the first group, Philip the second group, and James, son of Alphaeus, the third group. Such leadership suggests that he was a person of prominence, and quite possibly the writer of the Epistle bearing his name. Charles Fillmore relates James the Less, to the mind power or faculty of order; and the Epistle of James is very much in consonance with such an identification. The book is full of doctrine. In the second chapter of James, verses 10-12 emphasize the inviolability of the moral law. In chapter four, verses 1-3 sound a contemporary note, alluding to causes of war in the world and war within the individual, contention between the "haves" and "have-nots," and reaching past economic and political differences to psychological and emotional causes. In the first six verses of chapter five the writer calls down wrath upon frivolities, dissipations, war profiteering, and hoarding. If ever a man was for law and order, it was James.

But because we cannot get a positive response to the request, "Will the real James, son of Alphaeus, please stand up," perhaps we could concede the last word to A. Milton Smith, who offers this practical thought for these times: "James is the patron saint of the unrecognized and uncrowned. We look upon Peter as being the patron saint of the preachers, John of the mystics, Paul of the theologians, Andrew of the personal workers; but James is the patron saint of the unrecognized. Thousands fall in this class. They serve the Lord and support the cause, but since they are not gifted they are clouded in obscurity. . . . The majority of us will never do anything so outstanding as to command wide recognition. It is heartening to us to see that we are represented among the Twelve."

Simon, the Cananaean

Matthew referred to him as "Simon, the Cananaean." Luke described him as "Simon who was called Zealot." Both titles tell us a bit more than meets the eye, for while this Simon did live in Canaan, so did the eight other Simons named in the New Testament; therefore to call this one a dweller in Canaan would be no identification. It is evident that the appellation has another significance. The King James Version uses the term Kananite, which refers to a political party whose aim, as an underground movement, was to overthrow the rule of Rome in Canaan and transfer political power to the native people. Thus the new English Bible translates the passage, "a member of the Zealot party." The Phillips translation gives it, "Simon the Patriot." Dummelow refers to him as "the zealot," and elaborates on this: "The Zealots were a sect founded by Judas of Gamala (or of Galilee, Acts 5:37) who headed the opposition to the census of Quirinius, in A.D. 6 or 7. They bitterly resented the domination of Rome, and would fain have hastened with the sword the Messianic hope. During the great rebellion and the siege of Jerusalem their fanaticism made them terrible opponents, not only to the Romans, but to other factions among their own countrymen."

As modern Truth-seekers, interested in knowing something about the twelve powers of mind which we all possess, what difference does it make who Simon was?

Only that most of us want to know the reasons why he and other disciples are compared to such attributes. And here we trace such a relationship.

To human thought Simon was a poor prospect as a lightbearer of His message to all the nations of the world; as unlikely a prospect as the calling of twelve faculties to serve the Creative Principle in each of us! But Jesus judged His chosen not by what they were at the moment of being called to His service, but by what they were capable of becoming, and what therefore He could call forth in them. So it is with each of us.

We cannot wisely label one attribute good, another bad. Any of them is good for us when it is under control or dominion, bad when otherwise. It's like jam. On bread, we call it good. On a carpet, we call it bad. But the good and bad are in relation to our use of it, not the thing itself which is neither good nor bad, but jam.

Zeal, like so many other qualities of the human spirit, is a two-edged sword. Without a quota of zeal there is little ventured, little growth and progress. Too much of it can take the turn that "the end justifies the means," and produce a Hitler.

"Did Elijah overcome death, and take his body into the next dimension, the same as Jesus did, only 'in a chariot of fire'?" a student once asked Charles Fillmore.

"No," he answered. "Elijah's zeal consumed his house!"

Thaddaeus

"The personalities of Scripture represent mental attributes in the individual," says Charles Fillmore. He relates the person known as Thaddaeus to the mind power or quality of renunciation and/or elimination. It is interesting to consider the reasons for the comparison, as well as the importance of renunciation or elimination.

Thaddaeus was one of the Twelve, and like some of the others he was known by more than one name. Luke, in his Gospel and in The Acts, calls him Judas; John refers to him as "Judas, not Iscariot"; Mark calls him Thaddaeus. Matthew, in the King James Version, calls him "Lebbaeus, whose surname was Thaddaeus."

Only one utterance of this disciple is quoted in the Gospels, and that in John 14:21,22, when he asks Jesus, "How is it that you will manifest yourself to us, and not to the world?" Jesus answers to the effect that God will love those who keep His commandments, and will manifest Himself to them, but those who do not so love Him will not keep His word, and so He does not become manifest to them.

Most scholars identify Thaddaeus-Lebbaeus-Jude as the writer of one of the shortest books of the Bible. It comes just before The Revelation, and is so short that you might easily miss it entirely. If you do, you will also miss one of the sternest admonitions to renunciation and elimination of worldliness to be found anywhere, which offers us a connecting link between the disciple, Thaddaeus, and the mind power, renunciation and/or elimination.

When the Scriptures say, "it came to pass," no doubt the intent is to say "it occurred," but the truth is that all things come to pass; that each experience, each association, each lesson, has its place and purpose. They come to pass. Only what we have learned from them endures. But often we view this process fearfully, because we view it so closely and so personally. We cannot willingly renounce or eliminate. "We cannot part with our friends. We cannot let our angels go. We do not see that they only go out, that archangels may come in," says Emerson. And again, "The man or woman who would have remained a sunny garden-flower, with no room for its roots and too much sunshine for its head, by the falling of the walls and the neglect of the gardener is made the banian of the forest, yielding shade and fruit to wide neighborhoods of men."

Judas Iscariot

There is a way that seems good to mankind, the end of which is destruction. When we think of Judas Iscariot, his story seems to be almost epitomized in that one sentence. He was from the land of Moab in Judaea; the only one of the Twelve who was not a Galilean. The disciples have been called "the men whom Jesus made." Judas was no less promising in the beginning than any of the other disciples. He has the dubious distinction of being the only one whom Jesus could not make, or transform.

He was as intelligent as any of them. He had the same opportunities. They questioned and doubted perhaps no less than he, but they did not think that they knew more than He, as Judas did—to the point of betrayal.

In a way the story of Judas parallels the story of Adam and Eve. Allegorically the serpent that tempted Eve was sensual desire, the forbidden tree of the knowledge of good and evil. "If you eat of this tree," she and Adam were admonished, "you will surely die." But desire in the form of a serpent answered, "You will not die." Response to this desire, "eating the fruit of the tree," evicted the pair from the Garden of Eden where they abode in bliss, and projected them into the mundane world where they were to live by the sweat of their brows and learn through experience, as a result of demanding to have their own way.

At last, after the day that is as a thousand years, mankind begins to question his own way, and to think again that there must be and is a better way. They begin to "turn again home," in aspiration at least.

Judas, we are told, was the treasurer of the Twelve. He carried the moneybags. With his shrewdness of mind, it seemed to him that Jesus was not making the most of His opportunities. In the beginning of His ministry He might easily have claimed an earthly throne, become the long-awaited Messiah of the Jews. Judas was not alone in expecting and looking forward to this outcome. John and James, we recall, were concerned about who would sit at His right and left when He came into His kingdom. He told them that His kingdom was not of this world. It was at this point that their faith wavered—wavered, but did not cease. Even then Judas did not, from his own point of view, reject the Christ. He just thought that *he* knew better how to manage things.

If he were seemingly to betray the Master, put

Him in a position where His mission and His life were both endangered, He "would not die." He would simply wave a magic wand, say a magic word, wave a regal hand, and His enemies would fall, vanquished at His feet; the promised kingdom would appear, and they, the Twelve, would be the first ones to enter it.

It did not work out that way. Jesus was not swayed from His method or His purpose. He died on the cross, and rose in triumph from it. Judas, overwhelmed by his own treachery and its tragic outcome, went out and hanged himself.

God has given us a priceless gift, the gift of life. Scientists think that one day they will be able to create it themselves, without Him; but if they ever succeed in creating it, it will be because of Him. Meantime, that gift is also a responsibility.

"There is a way that seems good to mankind, the end of which is destruction." We need not look afar to see that this is so. The fruits of selfishness, greed, self-gratification are everywhere evident.

"Earnestly desire the higher gifts. And I will show you a still more excellent way," is the assuring word of that latterday apostle, Paul. It may lead us to discover the law above laws.

Mind Stretchers

Some of the world's greatest inventions and discoveries—all of them perhaps—began with a theory: Suppose that thus-and-thus were so. And because we live not only in a world of three dimensions, but perhaps more deeply and truly in a world of intangibles, a bridge of theory now and then may help us span a gap of unfinished thought.

The term *theory* should not be used in scorn. We live by the grace of the Creative Principle: God. We explain this by *facts* and *theories,* two words that are sometimes interchangeable.

Ideas, notions, concepts, press in upon us, out from within us, as if from some other dimension of being; and indeed this world of three dimensions is not self-explanatory. We have to take some things for granted that just do not make sense, if we endeavor to justify them on the basis of a three-dimensional concept of existence. Two such factors in human experience are time and space. Neither one makes sense. We cannot tell where time goes. Does the past exist? Does the future exist? If so, where? What of space? There is a very great deal of it. Where does it end? And if it ends, what is spacelessness like?

Herewith, then, we offer some concepts that are strongly supported by their advocates as being part of eternal truth; strongly rejected by others as fallacious; and tolerantly or even eagerly considered by still others, as offering possible answers to what materialists might call enigmas.

The Last Enemy

There is, so we are told, only one fear, the fear of death. This fear assumes many guises, but remove its masks and you will find that it is the same old fear.

Death, Paul said, is the last enemy to be overcome; but though death may be the last, fear is the greatest, and through overcoming fear we shall at last overcome death also.

We cannot live to our fullest capacity of joy and richness so long as the specter, Fear of Death, haunts the feast of our daily life. We are not living the overcoming life if we are living in the fear of death, or if we are living in fear at all. Fear is a paralyzing influence. Even in our dreams a clutching fear reduces us to helplessness. In our waking state it hampers our achievements.

Should we then fear nothing? Do not many things rightly command our fearful awe? Yes, our awe, perhaps, but not our *fearful* awe; our respect, unquestionably, but not our craven terror. There is that in us which is greater than anything that we may fear—greater, even, than death. When we find, and have gained confidence in, that greater something, we shall respect power wherever we find it, but we shall do so without the abject terror of the craven. Through finding our inner power we shall overcome fear, and through our newly-found courage we shall overcome the last enemy.

Perhaps we shall find too that death itself is not so much an enemy as is the fear of death; shall find that, when we have slain fear, we have thereby vanquished the enmity of death as well.

It is well to remember one Man who so thoroughly overcame the fear of death that He overcame death also, and rose, phoenixlike, from the ashes of death. He quickened His broken body to new life, and uplifted it to so high a state of purity and so subtle a responsiveness to Spirit that it became invisible to the gross eyes of sense, and now can be seen only through the finer senses of the inner man.

If a man die, shall he be born again?

Must we, then, surely die?

What can we believe of those that "sleep"?

These are questions asked by every generation of men, and answered variously according to the understanding of those who ask. The answer is not to be found in the study of death. We shall never find the knowledge of life by dissecting dead bodies in search of it. We shall not find the immortal spirit of man in the tomb. We must seek the knowledge of life in life.

If a man die, shall he be born again? He not only shall be, but he is!

Which Is You?

Where is the infant that once you were? He became a child, you say. Where, then, is the child? He has become the youth. The youth? He has become the man. Which one of these persons, so different in thought, action, appearance, are you? You are the one with whom you identify yourself, are you not? When you were a child, you spoke as a child, you felt as a child, you thought as a child. Now that you are full-grown, you have put away childish things. (See I Cor. 13:11.) You no longer speak, feel, or think in terms of that child. You no longer identify yourself with him. You have become a man. Did you have to die to become a man? Did you have to die to become a child and a youth? Did you have to die, perhaps, even to be born? Yes, in a certain way you have died many times, and are likely to die many times more, as often as you cease to identify yourself with one form of expression and assume another. Paul said, "I die every day."

The self of you that is observing these changes, that persists in spite of them, does not die. That self constantly seeks greater expression, and each new expression works changes in outward form. You let go certain limitations, you evolve more expansive ideas, and you clothe yourself with a form suited to these ideas. But whether you are clothed in the body of a babe, or a child, or a youth, or a man, you are you. You do not lose your identity, even though you become identified with a different appearance.

You put on your wraps to go downtown. When you return home you remove them. You are still the same individual. Were you wholly unclad, even to the point of losing your body, you would still be the same individual, and you would clothe yourself anew with a body that would express your evolving idea of yourself.

You cannot die in the sense of ceasing to be. You can die only in the sense of losing your body; and because you continue to live, you will continue your progress from the point at which you left off, and will rear a new body, perhaps a finer one. You will continue to grow and to evolve, and to change outwardly as you change inwardly. Eventually, we believe, you will have purified your mind, and also have learned to purify your body, to such a degree that you will not need to relinquish it to corruption, but can quicken it to spiritual expression as did Jesus the Christ.

To uplift the body into spiritual expression, instead of relinquishing it to death and corruption, may seem to us a far cry. It may even seem to be an impossible ideal. We grant you that the evidence for failure to do it is abundant, and that the assertion that some persons have duplicated the feat of the Christ in overcoming death, even though it might be warranted, would nevertheless be very difficult to prove. Stories have come to us out of the East that tell of spiritually illumined men who have never seen death; men who have lived in their bodies for hundreds of years, and have then simply disappeared without leaving any trace of their bodies. These stories may be legendary; but, if they are, they are nevertheless true to principle, and are in that sense prophetic of what mankind shall yet attain.

The best authority for belief in survival after death is the persistent desire to live. Desire is prophetic of its own fulfillment.

Nothing is ever lost in nature. Matter changes form, but it does not cease to exist. Apparently it cannot be destroyed. We can assume (if we do not know) that this is no less true of that which animates matter.

It is well for us to become satisfied regarding the persistence of life—to become satisfied, and then to dismiss the matter from our mind, and live. The purpose of existence is more important than the process; the purpose gives birth to the process, and that which produces is greater than that which is produced. The builder is greater than what he builds. The thinker is greater than his greatest thought. You are greater than what you think, what you build, what you express. The purpose of life is to express, in ever greater degree, that which you eternally are. That which you eternally are has never begun to be and can never cease to be.

The Eternal Self

That which you eternally are cannot be overcome by what it expresses or by what it fails to express. So long as it seems to be overcome, it has not yet fully found itself. So long as we are overcome by death we have not yet fully found our power.

As yet, humanity is overcome not only by death, but also by many other "enemies." Man allows himself to be overcome by lack, by disease, by unhappiness. To overcome these enemies should be his first concern. Let him satisfy himself that he eternally exists, that he cannot be annihilated by any of his enemies–even the last one–and he is prepared courageously to set about overcoming all his enemies. They are his enemies only so long as he fears their mastery of him. When he learns to make them serve him, they cease to be enemies.

Someone has said that weeds are simply plants out of place, or for which no one has yet found a use. Perhaps all the noxious things of life are simply good things out of place, or for which we have not yet found a constructive use.

Surely, until we shall have mastered the lesser enemies, the last enemy is a kind of friend. If we have not mastered one or more of the lesser enemies, and by our mistaken thought and action our body temple has become pain-wracked and unclean past our present understanding to redeem, then how great is the mercy that provides that we may slip out of it and try again!

God's plan for man is life: life eternal, life of body, soul, (mind) and spirit, harmoniously functioning as one; the city foursquare, the New Jerusalem of the Christ man. Any plan that fails to express this completeness fails to express perfection. For the most part, man has not yet accepted this plan as an ideal, much less as a workable plan of life. He still sees himself separated from his ultimate good, separated from God, separated from others; and this sense of separation, when carried to its ultimate, separates him from his body, depriving him of a vehicle through which to express the life that is God's gift to him.

Man has identified himself with existence apart from his good. He has thus fallen short of the mark or goal of life, God's life. Another name for this falling short is sin, and "the wages of sin is death." How often we have heard that statement quoted! But do you know equally well the passage that follows it, "But the free gift of God is eternal life in Christ Jesus"?

The free gift of God is eternal life! With that conviction securely established in our mind and heart, the attainment of that eternal life ceases to be the heavy burden that otherwise it might be. In the assurance of the life and power that we have within us, we find new inspiration, new courage, new strength and power. It is this message, more than any other, that Christ Jesus gave to the world.

Eternal Life in the Body?

"There is no death in the plan of God, God is life and love and joy. Man was not born to die but to live, to progress toward the goal of perfection. The cause of death and its entire experience lies in the consciousness of man, and not in the will of God. Eternal life means continuous conscious existence in the body. Man will attain eternal life when he perfects his consciousness."

Life is a continuum. Birth and death are events in the midst of life. We are continually dying and being reborn in the somatic or bodily sense. We die to the body of infancy and are born to that of childhood, we die to childhood and are born to youth, from youth to maturity, and so on through the years. Paul declared, "I die every day," and we might well add, "and daily I am reborn," for it is a fact of human experience. He also said, "the body does not consist of one member but of many," but probably even Paul did not realize how many members. We assume that by the many members he meant hands and feet, and the various bodily organs. But modern science would give another meaning to Paul's words. For we now know that the body has indeed many members; it is like a universe, even a galaxy, within itself, composed of myriad tiny bodies that have their little lifespans, their births and deaths and replacements, so that in a short space of time all its elements are renewed; and in this quite literal physical sense it may be said that we have died and been born again. Yet it has not harmed us but rather helped us, for it does seem to have been the intention of the Creative Forces of being that we should be always infants or little children or even youths—but we "must be born again," as Jesus tried to explain to Nicodemus.

Life goes on, even into other dimensions of being. "This perishable nature must put on the imperishable, and this mortal nature must put on immortality . . . then shall come to pass the saying that is written: 'Death is swallowed up in victory. O death, where is thy victory? O death, where is thy sting?' "

But now is the acceptable time, and the kingdom of heaven is at hand if we but have the consciousness to discern it. "Cast away from you all the transgressions which you have committed against me, and get yourselves a new heart and a new spirit! Why will you die, O house of Israel? For I have no pleasure in the death of any one, says the Lord God; so turn, and live."

We are to overcome death, not by dying, or by trying to overcome death, but by living. In the relative sense, we are related to the temporal world; we are continually growing, learning, overcoming, being born, and dying. In the eternal sense we are children of God and heaven, and the perfect, the heavenly, the ideal world interpenetrates this objective one. John tells about it in the Book of The Revelation when he says: "Then I saw a new heaven and a new earth; for the first heaven and the first earth had passed away, and the sea was no more. And I saw the holy city, new Jerusalem, coming down out of heaven from God, prepared as a bride adorned for her husband, and I heard a great voice from the throne saying, 'Behold, the dwelling of God is with men. He will dwell with them, and they shall be his people, and God himself will be with them; he will wipe every tear from their eyes, and death shall be no more, neither shall there be mourning nor crying nor pain any more, for the former things are passed away.' "

The Body Idea

Shall we retain the body we now have? Has the perishable put on the imperishable? Perhaps this is a major part of our unfinished work of the kingdom-come, for certainly we would not want to retain forever a body that is less than perfect. "If the creation seems to fall short of the divine perfection in any way, that is our fault," says Charles Fillmore.

"Either we are not seeing the whole or we are lacking in understanding. . . . God creates first in idea; His idea of creation is perfect, and that idea exists as a perfect model upon which all manifestation rests. The body of man must rest upon a divine body idea in Divine Mind, and it logically follows that the inner life, substance, and intelligence of all flesh are perfect. . . . Every person has a perfect body in mind; it is bringing itself into manifestation just as fast as he will let it, just as fast as he perceives God in the flesh."

This idea-body is the eternal body of man, as much a part of him as soul or spirit, and when conditions in consciousness are prepared, it will manifest. Perhaps all God's creations have such a characteristic body form. Consider, for instance, the combination of elements, H_2O. We identify it as a liquid, water; a gas, steam; a solid, ice. And when conditions are just right, in its crystal-like form as snowflakes. No other substance duplicates this form. It is exclusive to water. And no two snowflakes have ever been found to be exactly alike, though their form is so beautiful that they have been endlessly viewed and photographed. They are the crystalline form of water, as the idea-body of man is his distinctive Christlike (crystalline?) body.

Perhaps it was this idea-body that Peter, James, and John beheld in the transfiguration described by Matthew: "After six days Jesus took with him Peter and James and John his brother, and led them up a high mountain apart. And he was transfigured before them, and his face shone like the sun, and his garments became white as light. And behold, there appeared to them Moses and Elijah, talking with him." Peter suggested that he would make three booths or tabernacles to memorialize the occasion. "He was still speaking, when lo, a bright cloud overshadowed them, and a voice from the cloud said, 'This is my beloved Son, with whom I am well pleased; listen to him.' When the disciples heard this, they fell on their faces, and were filled with awe. But Jesus came and touched them, saying, 'Rise, and have no fear.' And when they lifted up their eyes, they saw no one but Jesus only."

Have We Lived Before?

Reincarnation is the rebirth of man in the physical body. It is the gospel of a second chance, man's opportunity to try again to embody more of his divine destiny of manifesting perfection. It is not a punishment, but rather a mark of the divine love of God. It is as if He were saying to us: "Here, my child. I will give you a fresh garment. You have another day, another opportunity. Go out from your Father's house into that strange country and do your best and be worthy of me. I will not fail you or forsake you. I will be with you and will guide you into the experiences through which you will learn and grow, and come to express what in My heart I have envisioned you to be."

Reincarnation is no more an ultimate of being than going to school is an ultimate. We go to school to learn things that will help us to exercise our dominion over our faculties of body, soul, and spirit in joyous living. When we have attained this self-mastery we will come in to "go no more out," as the King James Version of Revelation 3:12 expresses it.

What does the Bible say about reincarnation?

One of the notable allusions in the Old Testament is found in Proverbs, Chapter eight, verses 22 to 31:

"The Lord created me at the beginning of his work,
the first of his acts of old.
Ages ago I was set up,
at the first, before the beginning of the earth.
When there were no depths I was brought forth,
when there were no springs abounding with water.
Before the mountains had been shaped,
before the hills, I was brought forth;
Before he had made the earth with its fields,
or the first of the dust of the world.
When he established the heavens, I was there,
when he drew a circle on the face of the deep,
when he made firm the skies above,
when he established the fountains of the deep,
when he assigned to the sea its limit,
so that the waters might not transgress his command,
when he marked out the foundations of the earth,
then I was beside him, like a master workman;
and I was daily his delight,
rejoicing before him always,
rejoicing in his inhabited world
and delighting in the sons of men."

Solomon may have been referring to reincarnation when he said, "I am but a little child; I do not know how to go out or come in."

Malachi said, "Behold, I will send you Elijah the prophet before the great and terrible day of the Lord comes."

Jesus confirmed this prophecy when speaking of John the Baptist, He said, "And if you are willing to accept it, he is Elijah who is to come."

Again, Jesus asked the disciples, " 'Who do men say that the Son of man is?' The disciples answered, 'Some say John the Baptist, other say Elijah, and others Jeremiah or one of the prophets.' "

When the disciples referred to the prophecy that Elijah must come before "the Son of man is raised from the dead," He replied, " 'Elijah does come, and he is to restore all things; but I tell you that Elijah has already come, and they did not know him, but did to him whatever they pleased. So also the Son of man will suffer at their hands.' Then the disciples understood that he was speaking to them of John the Baptist."

The disciples, in another instance, were puzzled as to a man whom they observed had been born blind. "And his disciples asked him, 'Rabbi, who sinned, this man or his parents, that he was born blind?' Jesus answered, 'It was not that this man sinned, or his parents, but that the works of God might be made manifest in him. We must work the works of him who sent me, while it is day; night comes, when no one can work. As long as I am in the world, I am the light of the world.' "

How to Understand the Bible

"And they read from the book, from the law of God, clearly, [with interpretation]; and they gave the sense, so that the people understood the reading"–Neh. 8:8.

Through many stories the Bible tells one story, through many persons it tells of one person–you; through history, poetry, allegory, and symbolism it speaks the language of the body, soul, and spirit, to record the wanderings, the trials and overcomings, the defeats and victories of us all in this strange journey underneath the stars.

All the actors in the drama are one actor, man, and all the places are places that have been or shall be in your mind and heart. Remember this, and though sometimes you may feel lost as indeed most of us have felt in life itself, you shall find your way from confusion to understanding.

The story of the Bible begins with God; its very first words are, "In the beginning God:" And it ends with His manifestation in ideal human expression, which is the Christ of God: "He who testifies to these things says, 'Surely I am coming soon.' Amen. Come, Lord Jesus! The grace of the Lord Jesus be with all the saints. Amen." And in between is told the story of the incarnation of the sons of heaven upon the earth, with the clay of the earth still clinging to their feet and thought, and its stamp upon their life. Subject to all things, weighed upon by all, they had yet been endowed with that divine spark, breathed into them by the breath of God, which should fulfill the promise of their earthly beginnings.

When you read the Bible you are turning the pages of spiritual history. It is the story of aspiring man—his story. Read it with your God-given endowment of insight that enables you to see yourself in Adam, in Moses, in Jacob, in Joseph and Rachel, in Ruth and Esther; in Saul and David and Jeremiah, in Mary and Martha and Lazarus, in James and John—in Jesus Christ.

With Abram you shall ascend a high mountain and hear the voice of God telling you again of your dominion: "All the land which you see I will give to you." You shall feel the spirit within you questioning whether God wants you to give up whatever you deeply love, for Him whom you must love more.

With Abram you may fear that love of God means the sacrifice of what in you is Isaac, the joy of your life, only to learn with thanksgiving that better than to give up is to lift up in the dedicated life.

With John you may find yourself a voice crying in the wilderness of faith forgotten; with Peter you may sense the truth of man redeemed and coming into his kingdom, yet like Peter be many times faltering in faith and fealty. With Paul you may persecute the very thing you would embrace, and yet "breathing threats and murder" see a great light.

In all these ways and others, God's purposes are served. One by one you take them up and lay them down again, remembered and forgotten, until at last you shall glimpse the great and immortal possession which is yours of God, and claim it for your own.

Through all the warp and woof of this tapestry of life you shall discern, like a thread of gold, the interwoven pattern of God's plan for you.

The Law Above Laws

"By grace you have been saved through faith; and this is not your own doing, it is the gift of God"–Eph. 2:8.

"It is enough, that through Thy Grace,
I saw nought common on Thy Earth"–Rudyard Kipling.

If we have a knowledge of spiritual Truth should that not make us immune to the ills of the mundane world?

If we had attained to complete knowledge and understanding of spiritual Truth–and Truth is Truth whether we call it spiritual or otherwise–presumably we would have dominion in all things. But by the same token would we not therefore also have ascended into another dimension of being? In this plane of experience it is indeed difficult, perhaps impossible, to evaluate anything except in relation to its apparent environment.

Within the last century there has been a renaissance of the ancient wisdom, through various schools of advanced thought; of the law of equivalence, or cause and effect. To a culture that conceived the world to be governed by a Deity who could be cajoled by sacrifices, who demanded punishment for real or fancied sins, who could condemn His creatures to eternal damnation and torture, the viewpoint that we are punished not for our shortcomings, but by them, is an advancement of monumental proportions; an advancement only equalled by that made in the realm of material science.

"To outward appearance, the modern world was born of an anti-religious movement; man becoming self-sufficient and reason supplanting belief," says Teilhard de Chardin. "Our generation and the two that preceded it have heard little but talk of the conflict between science and faith; indeed it seemed at one moment a foregone conclusion that the former was destined to take the place of the latter.

"But, inasmuch as the tension is prolonged, the conflict visibly seems to need to be resolved in terms of an entirely different form of equilibrium—not in elimination, nor duality, but in synthesis. After close to two centuries of passionate struggles, neither science nor faith had succeeded in discrediting its adversary. On the contrary, it becomes obvious that neither can develop normally without the other. And the reason is simple: the same life animates both. Neither in its impetus nor its achievement can science go to its limits without becoming tinged with mysticism and charged with faith."

They are like the mind and heart of humanity, each valid in its own realm, and each in its own way stressing the universal nature of the law of action and reaction, cause and effect, equivalence, karma.

A press report quotes the nuclear scientist Dr. Wernher von Braun: "The two most powerful forces shaping our civilization today are science and religion. Through science man strives to learn more of the mysteries of creation. Through religion, he seeks to know more of the Creator."

The Human Predicament Again

Truth-seekers are often confused by an apparent

conflict between two valid viewpoints: one which asserts that there is but one Presence and one Power in the universe, God, the great Creative Principle; the other that sees life as composed of innumerable variables, relatively good, relatively evil.

The so-called absolute metaphysician attempts to surmount this impasse by asserting that there is no reality to evil, that all is good. But if he is really absolute must he not then include absolutely everything in his considerations? A problem is not solved simply by denying its existence, for everything is real on its own plane—though perhaps only a shadow of what is real in a higher dimension. Claude Bragdon offers this concept in his writings that deal with time-space and the fourth dimension. He suggests that the *shadow* of a human hand may appear to be the *reality* in a "flatland," or two-dimensional world, and that what is a real, living hand to us in this world of three dimensions is only "a shadow" of what is reality in a fourth dimension of being.

In a practical or pragmatic sense, we have to reconcile the apparent opposites. What is real? Webster's Unabridged Dictionary lists fourteen definitions; one of them is "fundamental and ultimate as opposed to merely apparent or phenomenal." In this sense we may say that evil has no reality, in the sense that it is apparent and phenomenal rather than ultimate and eternal.

Are not *good* and *evil* words that describe our reactions to conditions, relations, people, places?

Things are.

We call them good when they please us, evil when they do not. Often we find that as we progress toward higher attainment, the names for things become interchangeable or reversed—not necessarily for everybody, but for ourselves as individuals. "As for you, you meant evil against me; but God meant it for good."

Things are neither good nor evil, but thinking makes them so. They are opposites; cause and effect, positive and negative, male and female, action and reaction. We learn not to pass judgment. "Let not another's disobedience to Nature become an ill to you; for you were not born to be depressed or unhappy with others, but to be happy with them," said Epictetus. "And if any is unhappy, remember that he is so for himself; for God made all men to enjoy felicity and peace."

The Real and the Temporal

So we must learn to distinguish between that which is transient and that which is enduring. Evil is transient. Only good endures. Also in this reconciliation of opposites, we learn to distinguish between what people are and what they do. We may love them for the first, deplore them for the second; but we can learn to deplore only the sin, yet love the sinner. We can discern with the mind and heart what is denied by the senses: that back of even men's worst mistakes, his foulest crimes, there was the effort to bring about what seemed to the erring one a form of good either to himself or others, the elimination of some threat to life or love or trust. And if what he does offends you, take comfort in the thought that to recognize a shortcoming indicates that at least in vision and aspiration you have reached past it. Give thanks, and go on. A good sense of direction predicts attainment of a goal. Follow the gleam of light that flashes across the firmament of consciousness.

Why, having found a sense of direction, having perceived the light, is not attainment more rapid?

Although we are eternally sons of God and heaven, we have submitted ourselves to the discipline of experience, learning by trial and error, which are characteristic of this plane of manifestation. In a time-space world such as this, cause and effect are seldom simultaneous. Though conceivably in spirit results are instantaneous, to consciousness they are progressive. We experience things sequentially, *seriatim*. Thus, the bread of life, like the bread from the oven, is not to be bolted down in one gulp, but a morsel at a time, imbibed and digested. Not many persons are able to grasp the contents of a weighty book by sleeping with it under their pillow (as a few rare souls are reputed to do), or to absorb its contents by holding the printed volume between clasped hands. We may begin by reading it word by word, like a child. We progress to reading it line by line, page by page.

As long as we are in this plane of life then, reality is experienced relatively. We see as in a glass, darkly, though with dawning light. And if at times the problems we have invited, the challenges we face, the concern we feel for those we love, or for humanity generally, or the state of the world, seem too much for us, there is one law above laws that we can invoke.

It is the law of love, otherwise referred to as the law of grace; for grace means the gift of God. It is not something we have earned or can earn. It is God's free gift. Jesus alluded to it when He said that love is the fulfilling of the law. This saying may be one of the least understood of all the things He said, yet one of the most profound.

Without Bondage

Sometimes people think He meant that if you are loving you are not "under law." True, you will not be under *bondage* to the law, but the law will still exist, and you will bear some relationship to it: a deeper and a higher relationship. It means obedience not only to the letter of the law but to its spirit. It means becoming so immersed in the sense of God's love for you, that you in turn become more loving toward everyone and every condition that characterizes your world.

When you are ill or otherwise afflicted, there is obviously a cause for the condition. Things do not just happen: they result. "Putting men into uniform does not make uniform men." We are alike in general, we are different in particular. Superficially our reactions may be similar. Beneath generalities there are infinite variations. "What have I done that this should have come upon me?" is an instinctive acknowledgment of a relation between ourselves and our circumstances.

Whatever helps us in meeting the challenges of life is to that degree good, but there are occasions when any of what we think of as normal channels, meaning mundane ones, do not answer our need.

Invoke the law that is above laws, the law of grace.

You can do so by letting go all sense of bitterness, resentment, or injustice. Is there someone whom you wish to bless? Mentally enfold him in the love of God. Mentally see him as you conceive that he is in the sight of God. You are not trying to change anything. You are only clarifying your sight, to see him as God sees him. Has someone misunderstood you? Ask God to help you to communicate your good feelings. Have you misunderstood someone else? Do you have a sense of hurt feelings? No one can hurt you unless hurt was intended, and then only if you accept the hurt. Love casts out hurt feelings, dissolves them as shadows are dissolved before the light of the sun. "Tune in: turn on!"

Points of Light

The great Galilean said, "I am the light of the world." "You are the light of the world." "Let your light shine." In Him is the light of life, and in Him is no darkness at all. This is no mere metaphor. It is factual. It is truth. The chemical scientist, Dr. Donald Hatch Andrews, attempts to make this clear by inviting us to imagine ourself in the inner structure of an atom. It is composed of electrons whose number, arrangement, and rate of vibration give the atom its characteristic structure. "Since these electrons are moving very much like planets, you may ask whether there is anything corresponding to a sun at the center of the atom to hold these planetary electrons in their orbits . . . at the center you see a tiny whirling point of light."

Charles Fillmore had passed into a higher dimension before Dr. Andrews, with the precision of his chemistry-trained mind, wrote these words. But some forty years ago a student, sitting with a number of others in a meditation period lead by Mr. Fillmore, was puzzled by the fact that during meditation he felt much larger physically than his dimensions justified. He asked the teacher if there was some explanation for this other than imagination. The teacher's answer was that at the center of every cell and atom of the body there is a point of light. In the normal waking state, most of us do not activate this light energy. It is as if we are only partly "turned on," only partly awake, functioning at a fraction of our potential. In profound meditation the soul nature is stimulated, we "come alive." It is, he claimed, quite literally turning on more of the light that lights the life of every man coming into the world.

Turn inward then, in that direction which cannot be defined by the limitations of the physical senses. When we say "inward" we do not mean to the interior of the body, though as you think of the light that Jesus spoke of you may have a sense of warmth just below the heart in what is called the solar plexus (solar, of the sun; plexus, network or center) or sun center. Your thoughts and feelings evoke this bodily response, but do not become distracted by this fact. Do not resist it. Do not exaggerate its importance. Simply accept it, and dwell on the thought of light, light which is the light of your life, the light of the world, and silently affirm, *"From the center of light within me, I radiate love and healing to all the world. The light within me is one with the light of God, the light of Christ, the light of every man everywhere. It is a light of universal love and understanding, mighty to dispel the clouds of darkness that seem so real to human sense, mighty to bring peace, brotherhood and harmony into manifestation."*

UNITY SCHOOL OF CHRISTIANITY
Unity Village, Missouri 64065

Printed U.S.A. 107-F-2098-5M-5-77